Delere Press
The Screaming Series

Series Editor
Lim Lee Ching

This paperback edition first
published in 2018 by Delere
Press LLP, as part of The
Screaming Series.

The Technological Sublime
© Anders Kølle

First published in 2018 by
Delere Press LLP
www.delerepress.com
Delere Press LLP Reg No.
T11LL1061K

ISBN 978-981-11-7497-1

Art Direction by
Sarah and Schooling

THE
TECHNOLOGICAL
SUBLIME

THE
TECHNOLOGICAL
SUBLIME

ANDERS KØLLE

Delere Press

CONTENTS

A READER'S JOURNEY

The strange blend of naivety and unscrupulousness that has always characterized the coming into being of a book appears to have reached an end: Not that books are not written, read, and sold anymore – there are still believers, dreamers, pedants, and megalomaniacs among us – but the very significance of books has inevitably changed.
The book and the printing press were born of a spirit that related to the world in a twofold manner and assigned two clearly defined and separate roles: The creator, the author, the magician, the seer on the one side and the pupil, the apprentice, the listener on the other. This simplicity was unquestionably one of its great forces: One either knows or does not know yet, one either speaks or one listens, one has either already reached a destination or one is still on the way. The library could thus function as a place of transition: It was a place for the meticulous laying out of stepping-stones so that one might one day cross the divide. And it was a place of transformation: A womb for the slow growing of wings on the conscientious pupil – and of claws and teeth on the future conquistadors. To be a schoolmaster, a judge, a doctor or a professor meant fundamentally that one had not only read but also incorporated the canonical wisdom of one's field. Through the agreed authority of certain books one could become an authority as well – a new face on an old knowledge, a new incarnation of an established wisdom: Hence the towering bookcases and endless rows of books that used to decorate the offices of solemn and important men and women: Each title was

yet another jewel in the scepter and crown of knowledge, another step up the grand staircase of wisdom. To read was to ascend, to climb and rise upward. In a continuous movement – word by word, sentence by sentence, book by book – one distanced oneself from the world of mere matter and blind chance to approach a higher and ideal sphere of meaning and abstraction, logic and reason. Everything depended on this distance – the book itself was a promise of distance and a vehicle for continuous distancing: Whereas the illiterate was forced to live in the eternal proximity of things, with no route of escape from the bewilderments and derailments of his purely corporeal existence and un-orchestrated ideas, the literate had a chance to transcend the level of the immediate and to breath the clearer air of abstraction. From on high the world looked different: Nature appeared to answer to laws, chaos answered to ideas, flux answered to form. And indeed the scholar only rose still higher and distanced himself still further in order one day to turn around and look back and observe the object of his previous confusion and misconceptions – just as the mountain climber only strives for the summit to look down into the abyss, and the Greek hero, Orpheus, only looked back at his beautiful Eurydice in order to *win* her at the greatest possible distance. To move up to look down: Herein lay the very purpose of the scholar's trajectory and the idealism of the climb. The downcast gaze always carried this message: "I have moved beyond your reach and into the distance of the untouchables." Flickering and searching eyes – permeated with all the uncertainties and anxieties of existence – were supplanted by the stern gaze

Anders Kølle

of the detached knower. Knowledge was, in other words, inseparable from the gaze, and the gaze inseparable from the distance. Together the three constituted the power of objectivity as the triumph of reason over matter and as the revenge of ideas upon the impermanence of life. Before there was any love of wisdom, any actual *philosophia*, any natural or human sciences, there was therefore a profound dread of the world that prompted man to invent his own defense. Fear and not love, passion and not reason, escape and not ambition, were the true parents of the distanced and objective observer. Only later could man pretend that he had always sought wisdom for its *own* sake, because of his sincere and profound love of it; only later could he deceive himself into believing that he was especially gifted rather than particularly afraid. Hence this odd yet plausible hypothesis: What originally separated man from the animal was not his intelligence and rationality but his ignorance and anxiety. Instead of identifying one enemy or protecting himself from one danger, man saw danger and enemies everywhere: Waiting for him in the night, at sea, in the rivers and in the forests. He could do nothing and go nowhere without putting himself at risk. *All* of nature seemed determined to conspire against him and to have but one goal: To bring man down. Paranoia made man flee, megalomania made him run: Not in one single direction, not towards one specific place but away from anything and everything at the same time. Transcendence and illumination were just two of the euphemisms by which he named this panic. And seeing that no one followed him on his confused flight, he congratulated himself on his unique behavior and blamed the animal for its stupidity in staying where it was.

Panic, paranoia, megalomania and flight: From the deep caves of the human mind these feelings, distortions, and reactions have resonated for millennia and sculpted much of our celebrated thinking and literature. The galloping heart that was already Homer's and turned into the spectacular adventures of Odysseus! First lesson of the epos: You are safe nowhere. Everyone seeks just one thing: To deceive you, trick you, capture you, kill you. Believe in no one and always move on. Stop and observe only from a distance. Listen only from afar. No Western hero has perhaps been more fearful and paranoid than Odysseus. No character ever quite so certain of his own importance: From the god of the sea, Poseidon, and the witch-goddess Circe to Calypso, Scylla, and the Sirens he is the constant center of attention, desires, controversies, and resentment. But far from mocking and ridiculing him and exposing his preposterous self-aggrandizement, Homer does the very reverse: Every fear is justified by the events, all anxiety proved reasonable. And hence the spectacular transformation: Odysseus, the paranoid narcissist, is turned into the most *reasonable* of heroes. He becomes the savviest of all. Achilles, the brute force of nature, cannot but perish. He is too close to the old world – too much himself a part of nature. The new order belongs to the escape artist – the ever distrustful and homeless man. And so fear is masked by reason, dread is draped in judgment, and the fugitive reasserts his place as rightful King of Ithaca.

Anders Kølle

It is no coincidence, then, that the *Iliad* and the *Odyssey* are among the first Greek poems to be recorded and written down. And that the first *printed* book in history, the Gutenberg bible, recounts the spectacular journey of yet another famous hero and even greater escape artist, who began his life at the very bottom only to later rise high above us all. And also in this story the persecuted one turned out to be a king, the fugitive to be the master, the homeless to be rightfully seated on the throne. Transcendence lies from the beginning at the very heart of books. Eventually pain and fear are overcome but only through distance, only by flight. "Fear is my only lifelong passion," said Hobbes and wrote his treatise on the elevated *Leviathan* whose supremacy should make life among ordinary men tolerable and endurable. This is the escape that has been repeated in so many ways, dressed in so many guises. Genuine love of wisdom has always been secondary. Affection here is only comparable to the feelings a soldier has for his weapons and a vagabond has for his shoes. Dread is the true engine: The fruits of wisdom are not reached for with a steady hand but with the trembling and sweaty palms of panic. One needs only to peel off the most superficial layer of certitude and coolness of much philosophy to see the true depths of fear which hide underneath. The troubled minds of Kant, Hegel and Schopenhauer – or the great doubts and profound nervousness of Descartes with whom the history of modern philosophy itself began: Not with a victorious roar but with a timid and panicking tremor. What if there is nothing of which I can be certain? What if everything is illusion and deceit? Great fear and ignorance – not great knowledge and wisdom were the starting gun by which the modern race for shelter began. And the homeless philosopher, Descartes, found the same answer as his homeless predecessors: To conquer you must move away. To win you must ascend and observe from afar. Hence the mind was detached from matter, the spirit divorced from the body. By sacrificing the body to Mother Nature and letting her do what she wanted with it, man saved the best part for himself. No longer tied down by the vulnerability and plumpness of our flesh, thinking could rise freely on its own.

The illiterate as well as the picky and more skeptical readers have always suspected as much – they have always seen what the scholars, the bookworms, the men of letters take much longer to understand: That reading, escapism, and asceticism are closely knitted together, that the three of them constitute a genuine Borromean knot. If every book is a flight of the mind – the dream of supreme distance, the contemplation of still greater heights – then this very rising and liberation of the spirit necessitates a sacrifice that every serious and conscientious reader is obliged to make: the desire for earthly things, *cupiditas*, must be supplanted by a desire for the higher and the beyond, *caritas*. Every book thus confronts its readers with an ultimatum: "To approach me you must want me. And if you want me you must prove to me that you are sincere." This is the jealous message and silent claim that resounds from every bookshelf and meets the reader from every cover, title, chapter and page of his book. But how does one do that? How should this will and sincerity be expressed? How should they be shown and offered? The deafening silence and morgue-like ambience of so many private reading rooms and town hall libraries provide the answer: One pays with the sacrifice of one's body. This is the prize that all readers must pay. To read always means to immobilize oneself, to turn one's body into a statue of irresponsiveness and irreproachability. All purely corporeal needs and desires are either postponed or forsaken. The reader enters into a strange mimic performance where that which is imitated is nothing but death itself: The ultimate stillness and deepest silence that eventually conquer our noisy and restless bodies. But this seeming self-annihilation, this premature death of the flesh, is only what clears the way and prepares the ground for the crucial event: the resurrection of the mind! From the abandoned corporality springs the liberated and invigorated spirit. By turning his back on the world, by proving his readiness and ability to block out all external stimuli and denounce all inferior urges, the reader is already on his way to salvation: the long climb upwards which is the promised route of escape. No longer a victim of the world's unpredictability and of nature's endless cruelty, the reader can eventually smile and wave to both of them from above. He need not fear them any longer; he has moved beyond the reach of their conspiracies and their countless attacks. Now, from the heights of knowledge his mind has found a better home.

What a surprising and peculiar art form reading therefore is! Surely, to master the art of immobilizing one's body, of blocking out all external stimuli, of sitting absolutely still for hours and hours takes incredible discipline and many years of training. This training can therefore not begin early enough: All children of literate societies are subjected to the practice and discipline from the very first years of school. Sitting still is imprinted as a particularly important skill – a genuine virtue even. Children who master this skill early on are praised for their "good character" and "good behavior". Children who, on the other hand, do not easily comply with the demands and perform poorly in the art of immobilization are either subjected to corporal punishment – as a reminder precisely of the stumbling block that the body is regarded to be – or they are subjected to even more difficult and torturous exercises in immobility: To stand still in the corner of the classroom facing the wall instead of having at least a book to look at and a chair or a bench to sit on. These seemingly impossible and painful demands can only be justified by the profound belief broadly shared in literate societies that the elevation and illumination of the mind requires the restraint and confinement of the body. That indeed the liberation of the mind demands this sacrifice which every child must readily make in order to progress. In the end reading is therefore healthy rather than harmful, beneficial rather than cruel. One needs, however, only to imagine an illiterate individual who has never heard of books and has absolutely no concept of reading to see how strange and eerie this practice may look from the outside: In a great space with row after row of objects made of paper people are gathered and sitting about. But one hears no laughter, no cries, no mumbling, no talk. No one looks at or communicates with each other. One can hardly hear or see people breathe. A sacral space? A tomb of sorts? A church or a morgue? Or perhaps our illiterate friend would be reminded that in fact there are animals that at times display a similarly strange behavior: When in immediate danger, when the predator has come too near and there is no place to seek refuge, certain birds, snakes, frogs and mammals play dead. Singled out and with no other means of defense they simply pretend that they "are" no longer, that they have already "left". Does something similar explain the behavior of the people here? Similar it truly is: As if no bush or tree or rock was ever able to hide the oddity and eye-catching features of man he has always felt singled out and alone. His self-aggrandizement was the bitter fruit of his feeling of vulnerability. His imagination proportionate with his sense of exposure: Only a delicate border separates these two ideas: "I have no means of protection and no place to hide" from "Everyone is threatening my existence and looking to destroy me". Although our imaginary friend may therefore be unfamiliar with the practice of reading and with the strangeness of libraries, he may nevertheless have understood reading in its essence: Every book is a momentary shelter where man looks for his own and everlasting escape.

However much the reader fundamentally shares with the trapped animal and with the snake and the bird faking its own death, one crucial difference also separates and distinguishes them: Readers are the first to encompass the strange paradox that rest and movement are not incompatible, that fixation and locomotion can coexist.

Long before trains, cars, and planes in their own way proved them right, readers sought to embark on inner journeys covering entire mental landscapes, ascending towards ever higher peaks. In fact, even when the Age of the Enlightenment arrived with its notorious and pompous attacks on everything which could not be rationally explained, man's postulated ability to rise in the spirit and levitate himself was never questioned – his magical flight never included in the larger program of demystification and desacralization for which this age otherwise became so famous. On the contrary it appears that reading was even further glorified and sacralized by enlightenment philosophers: No being was considered quite as beautiful, no human being praised and adored quite as much as the splendid educated man, the supreme man of letters. Indeed one may even suspect that the enlightenment philosophers only attacked the old masters and dethroned the old kings and priests in order to replace them with a new and even mightier figure – the high priest of reason. This new priest would soon prove no less demanding and require no less respect and veneration than the old priests had done. In fact, he would feel entitled to much more: How effortless to repeat the gospels of others! How convenient to say what others have already said, dream what others have already dreamt. Hence this new gospel and song of glory: *Sapere aude* – dare to know. This was the gift that the new high priest had descended from his seat of wisdom to bring to the people. If you dare to know and if you dare to see through the hypocrisy of the old world and rise above the superstitions of uneducated men then you too shall be among the blessed and become one of the light-bringers of tomorrow. And yet, the question remained: know what? What precisely should one have the courage to realize? First of all this seductive answer: "know that you are free and that no one can take this freedom from you" - quickly followed by this strange and less seductive precaution and imperative: "And because you are free and because no one can tell you what to do, then listen to what I say and restrain yourself!" But however paradoxical, however disappointing in the end, it is impossible to ignore the true stroke of genius by which this new gospel was born. One must pause for a moment to discover the brilliant way in which *sapere aude* managed to invert everything and turn all motives and values upside down: From being the most frightened of beings, the most troubled and the most desperate to seek refuge, the man of letters now congratulated himself for being the most courageous and the most heroic of all. Now, the ones who did not follow in his footsteps, the ones who did not dare what he dared – those were the true cowards and the wretched of the earth. Pity the man who was afraid to know! Pity the man who kept himself out of the light! The future belonged to the brave. And so the bookworm was reborn a lion and the books became an emblem of courage and a symbol of endurance and fighting spirit: Like hunting trophies each title bore testimony to its reader's daring – the triumphs he had achieved and the obstacles he had surmounted. To cross the roaring sea of words and face knowledge wherever it hides – never afraid of a new insight, never shy away from a new idea. The reader had never been more impressive! And the books followed his level of ambition:

Voltaire's *Dictionnaire philosophique* which assembled all the philosopher's lifelong accumulation of knowledge, thoughts and opinions on everything from adultery, animals, and art to tears, tolerance and virtue; Diderot's *Encyclopédie* which aimed at nothing less than collecting all of human knowledge in its entirety – thirty-five volumes with the declared ambition to "change the way people think". But surely the word "change" was deliberately vague. Just as the volumes themselves were organized according to new principles – alphabetical order – so they also carried the desire for a new social organization and a new social order. This was the real "change" that the volumes aimed at: A re-stratification of the whole social domain so that this time the educated and the enlightened would come out on top. The sun kings of tomorrow should no longer be the privileged by birth but the privileged by knowledge. And since knowledge was *in principle* attainable, could be acquired by those who dared it and sought it, this new social stratification was no longer deterministic, no longer settled a man's destiny from the very outset, but offered the possibility of movement. Such was the promising and enticing dimension of the enlightenment project: To replace fixation with mobility, entrapment with potentiality. Education would provide every man with the means necessary to raise himself, to go beyond himself, to transcend himself and his inborn social position. For the hungry and the ambitious the new social hierarchy was no longer a trap but a ladder: One could climb it and rise as high as one dared. Those most hungry for light and least afraid of heights would meet no unsurpassable limitations. *In principle* the light of reason could be anyone's possession.

Anders Kølle

Even if these ideals of the Enlightenment remained thoughts and intentions rather than reality, they did place an engine of change under the static structure of the old order. Something could no longer be held back, something seemed bound to burst through. One little word describes the change: In early English use "progress" was the name of "a state journey of royalty". Now, it had a different meaning: Progress meant first and foremost growth and development. In a certain sense this was still a journey but a journey undertaken for the sake of the future, for the sake of becoming, of transformation and of transmutation. "All that is solid melts into air"[1] wrote Marx and Engels in 1848. But by then solidity had already been supplanted by the faith in changeability. There was no longer anything praiseworthy about remaining the same, nothing desirable in the repetition and the return. Everything that tradition and rituals had rested on, the very sanctity of identity and sameness, was broken beyond repair. Culture had to grow and evolve, business had to expand, art and science had to look for ever new expressions and results. Time itself seemed to have grown impatient, was constantly tapping its long fingers on the tables of tomorrow. For Enlightenment philosophers progress had been limited to a movement upwards: Their hierarchical thinking could show no other way: Necessarily darkness was at the bottom and light was at the top. What was true for the forest and the ocean was also true for man. But soon the very intoxication with development unfolded in every direction: forward and outward, inward and downward. Growth could no longer be limited to one single direction or one single dimension.

As eager as Voltaire and Kant had been to point to the lofty sky of reason others were now to bring man into the width and depth of existence. The *Bildungsroman* arrived as the very quintessence of a multidimensional growth. And it brought this strange and secretive message: Sometimes greatness hides in the miniscule, sometimes chance is the only necessity of life. Everything depends on one's ability to grow *with* life and one's capacity to grow *into* life. Existence itself then becomes a continuous birth: a perpetual call for self-creation and self-formation. But one does not change and evolve in order to become something finally settled, secluded, and self-enclosed. It is not the self as an autonomous work of art that is the goal. Rather, one grows and develops in order to meet life, to better understand life. For the one who does not understand remains at the outside: To him most incidents are insignificant and most encounters incidental. And any misfortune remains the result of bad luck. The violence of life as well as the gifts that it brings are always isolated accidents devoid of intent or purpose. Hence the man on the outside, life's illiterate passenger, is bound to an inconsequential existence. Not because his life *has* no meaning but because he is unable to *give* it one. It passes like everything else passes without leaving anything but certain scattered memories, marks and traces. Thus his true misfortune: He does not know how to *read* life but only *flips* through it precluding any signs and signification and any continuity and totality to ever emerge.

The *Bildungsroman* is essentially not a novel about life, but it is life itself that has become a novel. It tells us that one must become a reader of one's own existence in order to grow into its writer and creator. Progress therefore begins with decipherment and interpretation. Does that lift one upwards? Towards still greater comprehension and intelligibility? Not necessarily. First of all it renders every surface deep. Just as the pages of a book are only deep to the one who knows how to transform their signs into vehicles of understanding, so there can be no depth in general separate from the hieroglyphs of existence. From this perspective reading is not simply an escape or a flight towards light, nor is it a matter of domesticating by moving away, but it is an act that gives volume and renders deep by turning life into a series of signs. Chance encounters and random events may now prove to have their own hidden value and significance. They point beyond themselves and invite their reader to embark on a contemplative journey towards the very vanishing point of existence: The place where all the individual lines, events and traces finally meet – and where they simultaneously dissolve and disappear. Thus the *Bildungsroman's* emphasis on the voyage instead of on the resolution, the synthesis and the end. In the beginning there are still only meaningless surfaces and in the end there is once more nothing to be found. But on the way there are hieroglyphs that turn readable and open up their deeper secrets. On the way there is formation and growth and expansion. And on the way there are incidents that begin to resonate, events that begin to tremble and communicate and show their deeper coherency and connection. Goethe's Wilhelm Meister finds such a gravitational force in the face and figure of Mariane. Her image is at once a hieroglyph, a key, and a crossroad. From his first meeting with her she proves to incorporate the secret force that brings the disparate and discrete into contact. Now the different choices and separate accidents of life strike a deeper chord – turn voluminous and symphonic. The inaudible whispering that leaves a man perplexed and rejected gradually grows into sound, into harmony, into music. But this growth is in fact not a growth outside of Wilhelm, the music is in truth not external: Rather it is Wilhelm himself who is growing and changing. The illiterate passenger gradually becomes a reader of life's own score. This does not prevent mistakes and misreadings. The new reader still stammers and stutters. He reads too slowly and suddenly too fast. He jumps ahead when he should have stayed and stays when he should have jumped. Thus Wilhelm's love for Mariane is expressed both too soon and too late. It is hopelessly void of rhythm and proper intonation. Yet, these very mistakes are not simply accidents but treasurable lessons. Unlike the Greek tragedies there is meaning to be found in the misery and a promise to be heard in the failures: The world of the *Bildungsroman* is never a closed-circuit of inescapable destinies and unreasonable fate. Instead every failure and obstacle contains an invitation to its own surpassing and a key to its own overcoming: Make it a readable sign, make it signify and resonate and the misery will lead to progress instead of arrestment. Creon and Oedipus the King were still too poor readers to be anything but spectators to their own tragic lives. But the hero of the *Bildungsroman* changes and evolves throughout: One lesson leads to the next as naturally as chapters in a book follow each other. The reader matures with the text. At the end all stammer and misreadings are replaced by the comprehension of the evolved and fluent reader. The signs connect effortlessly and carry meaning from one passage to the next. Disparate semantic islands are brought together and onto common ground. No more fragments and sharp edges, no dyslexic scattering stands in the way. A whole is emerging and unites across all fault lines, accidents and disruptions. Everything is now a part of the same totality and can be assigned its proper role and place. But this is also where the journey and the book must necessarily end: Not with a spectacular climax but with a deep and lethargic silence. When all signs have been read and deciphered, when all lines and events have found their shared direction and denominator, they inevitably turn mute. Growth itself must in the end grow mute – the final resolution is pure dissolution: Death.

Is the *Bildungsroman* still a way of mastering life? Is evolution still a question of control and growth still a way to govern? Is the underlying and fundamental dread of existence, in other words, unaltered but only the solution and direction different? The answer is not univocal but ambiguous and dual: Both yes and no. Yes, since the fluent reader of life's own signs is inevitably also life's domesticator and tamer: Where there was initially pure contingency there gradually comes perspective, where there were only accidents and confusion there come coherence and understanding. Hence the tone of optimism that insistently drives the narrative forward: Life may not be readable at first, you may not immediately be able to understand it. But be patient and it will eventually give in. Then matter becomes form, form becomes sign, and sign becomes meaning. No longer a stranger to life, no longer its hostage and victim, you grow deep and experienced enough to embrace it one day. At the end nothing can startle you, nothing can surprise and upset you: Everything is assimilable, digestible, interiorizable and everything will find its proper place and importance in the spacious and inclusive mind of the evolved reader. And yet, this optimism, this final grandness of the intellect and of the soul and their all-encompassing powers is rarely depicted without some reservation, without at least a tint of either doubt or irony. Although Schiller may have been able to believe sincerely and naively in the ultimate education of man, Goethe's own position is in fact less easily discerned. One feels compelled to ask: Is Wilhelm *Meister* really worthy of his name? Does he in fact grow to become a true master? Or is his final mastery more an empty postulation than a fact – more theatrics and role-play than truth? Which also amounts to asking: Does Goethe really believe in his fiction – or does he only believe in the reality of his own make-belief? Hence the uncertainty, hence the ambiguity: Yes, there is attainable knowledge and yes, there is both development and growth. But to what end and to what degree? Isn't it also true that life inevitably leaves something unsolved? Something which despite all attempts remains undecipherable and indiscernible? And shouldn't this perhaps be the final lesson? Then silence does not simply replace the buzz because the world is left with nothing more to say – rather the final

Anders Kølle

silence results from their being something which cannot be said. Something indigestible by nature, an otherness that retains its mystery and secrets: as a cryptogram without a code or as a force devoid of meaning. Whatever Goethe's own position may have been the early Romantics were less ambiguous and opted unhesitatingly for the latter interpretation: There are limits to human interiorization and assimilation. Not everything answers to man's call for knowledge and meaning. But these apparent shortcomings and limitations are not regrettable or deplorable but worthy of both awe and celebration: Since some questions may forever be unanswerable to man, his search, his desire and his progress will themselves be endless. His growth will not stop but perpetually reach for the highest and deepest secrets. Imperfect as man is, he becomes infinitely perfectible and life's eternal apprentice. What fun, greatness or glory is there in being the master anyway? Are not all masters profoundly boring? Better to be a traveler of the mind and a vagabond of the spirit than a settler and a colonizer. The latter puts up fences whereas the former transgresses against them. What seems most appealing: To protect or to discover? To stagnate or to grow?

Romantic irony is therefore both a continuation and an alteration of the *Bildungsroman*. What it continues is the valorization of progress and what it postpones is the final resolution and death. Something that neither the Enlightenment thinkers nor any of their predecessors had been able to appreciate is now unearthed and brought into the very center of attention: The beauty of darkness and the treasure of ignorance. How magnificent is not the abyss! How splendid the vertigo! To fall head first into the unfathomable mazes of nature: no Ariadne's thread to save the diver but pure intoxication and ecstasy. To lose oneself in the greatness of the miniscule: Isn't infinitude everywhere around us? In the intricate filigree of a simple leaf? In the astonishing beauty of a rose petal? So delicate and timid, yet so majestic and vast. For the one who is no longer steered by the voice of reason alone, who is not in a hurry to reach the light, there are great chasms of secrets and deep clefts of wonder opening in every direction. Life is not simply signs to be deciphered and nature not only a code to be broken: More important than meaning is amazement and more essential than order is depth. If the early Romantics can indeed still be called readers, they undoubtedly constitute a new and different type of reader with a new and surprising ambition and goal: Not to be fluent and confident but to be hesitant, wavering, and slow. However strange and irrational this ambition may seem it is perfectly congruent with the core Romantic ideals and its most fundamental lesson: There is not much value in coming quickly and safely to the end. The one who swiftly proceeds down every passage and easily connects all signs may well have overcome the road but he will have lost the thrill of the journey – he may have gained knowledge but he will have bypassed the gateways to wisdom. Reading then means taking a risk. Less a discipline to be mastered it is an invitation to get lost. When the signs are no longer stable and their meaning is no longer fixed, the possibility of adventure and unpredictability opens up. Endless realms of unknown territory await the explorer within and beyond the immediate and apparent. Hence their approach and willful amateurism: Leave room for surprise and set aside time to be baffled. Let the signs tremble and flicker and always give something the chance to slip away.

What the Romantics fear is therefore no longer ignorance and obscurity but rather perfect transparency and self-evident, exhausted truths. Should everything one day be clear then what would there be left to hope for? Or should everything one day be grasped then what would there still be to reach for? Unending growth requires unending horizons. The desire of the Enlightenment thinkers to solve every mystery and capture every meaning thus appears menacing and destructive rather than wholesome and sound. For ideas need shadow as much as they need light and thoughts need obscurity as much as they need facts. Thus the Romantic reversal of the Enlightenment ideal: To approach the unknowable and indiscernible instead of the solvable and decipherable. Not to dare knowledge but to dare ignorance and uncertainty. *Tenebris aude*! Herein lies undoubtedly a much greater and deeper challenge to the human mind. And only where man finds this courage does he also find the key to unending progress. For every adventure he grows deeper, for every secret he grows wider. The human soul itself must constantly expand in every direction and become plastic and transmutable: To reach for one truth it must grow wings and to reach for another it must develop talons. Some strange whisper asks for ears which are no longer human and some grand visions require eyes which can see into the night. A new sensibility and a new sensitivity go hand in hand with the novel Romantic ideal. The Romantic hero is a polysensory and polymorphous being: Ever open to the impressions of the world and the tremors of the ground his soul is constantly moved and altered. Schlegel's aphorisms and irony express this changeability well: One moment he registers the sweetness of a sonata and the next he picks up on the noise from a sour literary critic or on the smell of badly written poetry. The text can no longer be coherent and fluid since the world itself is fragmented and inconsistent. Nothing can therefore connect across all divides and bridge all differences. In fact, the truly sensitive soul knows that it makes little sense to talk about *one* world at all. What would this *oneness* consist in? What should the great gathering force be? Emotion intuits what reason fails to conceive: Life is not coherent or continuous but it is becoming, alteration and unpredictability. The great wholeness of existence is what Romantic sensibility can therefore no longer retain. But the loss of perfect harmony and unity can only be mourned with crocodile tears - something far more interesting and challenging has replaced it: Unending worlds of wonder and infinite human perfectibility.

To summarize the trajectory traveled so far: First hypothesis: There is an attempt to escape from chaos, an attempt to ascend and rise above the contingency of nature and life's inexplicable cruelty. Literature came into being as an answer to the challenge of life itself and fostered the image of the escape artist as a gift to anxiety-ridden humanity. But to

Anders Kølle

receive the gift a price had to be paid: The rising of the spirit demanded the sacrificing of the body and the reader was born as the very epitome of this ultimatum: Man gains his distance and his freedom by immunizing himself to the noise and restlessness of the flesh. Every reader is, from this perspective, an Odysseus who has tied himself to the mast. Desire of earthly things is defeated by a striving for higher goals: The purer sphere of abstraction and the elevated realm of ideas. Hence the first, primordial naivety as well as unscrupulousness of the reader: At a distance the world becomes clear. And once it is clear it can be taken into possession. What eluded the illiterate becomes an object of manipulation for the literate. An organized, systematized, and categorized nature is the way enlightened man finally takes his revenge. No longer simply forced to react and adapt he assigns himself the role of commander. Second hypothesis: In addition to a striving upwards and towards clarity and mastery there is a movement in depth and towards continuous progress and growth. By this second movement and vector another direction of being as well as another set of values and another type of reader are produced: Not only the escape but also the dive, not only reason and discipline but also seduction and sentiment are quintessential literary motives and forces. Life, then, is no longer an object to be mastered from afar but an invitation to develop and evolve: Either with the aim of growing deep enough to encompass it – the reader's and decipherer's ideal and ultimate depth where all riddles and signs finally find their meaning and importance – or with the aim of fostering infinite growth

– self-formation and transmutation beyond the scope of coherency and conclusive synthetization. Now, when placed in opposition these two vectors or directions of reading would allow us to understand the rivalry and power struggles which have perpetually swept and divided the scene of literature: How the stammer and sentimentality of the poet has always been met with ridicule and mockery from the self-declared rationalists and self-aggrandizing realists: Why all these derailments and accidents? Why taste and suck on language as if it was a piece of candy melting on the tongue? Is it anything but mannerisms and affectation? Linguistic tricks to impress and corrupt the docile and weak-minded? Or the repugnance and bitterness that have prevailed through centuries between the man of faith and revelation and the man of facts and empirical interrogation: Each charges the other with making it much too easy and convenient for himself. Each is persuaded that the other cheats in the race to the top: One by neglecting to face reality and the other by refusing to see the Truth. Between such extremes, all kinds of quarrels and disputes repeatedly irrupt: The passion for words versus the respect for ideas, the menace of univocality against the threat of ambiguity, the struggle for meaning against the play of signification. But what the internal rivalry and perpetual battles between different readers and scholars obfuscate is that despite all divergences and incommensurables, despite all mutual alienation and animosity, there is also something that they share – something which is so deeply ingrained in the act of reading itself that it appears almost superfluous to mention it: Reading makes a change! Reading makes the

Anders Kølle

reader change! This both the diver and the escape artist agree on. Somehow, one is not the same when one begins and when one finishes a book. In between, through the act of reading, a difference will occur. And, in the end, it is precisely for this difference, *in the name of this difference*, that reading is desirable. Whether one seeks to ascend or wishes to grow deeper, whether one prefers the Bible over myths or one loves Shakespeare more than Goethe, the belief that reading produces something new is persistent. Hope, then, is in fact the uniting feeling: Hope that I too may travel, hope that I too may find release! If every nightmare is circular and all despair is repetitive then the book with its linearity promises to break the claustrophobic orbits: From sentence to sentence and chapter to chapter – like railway lines across Siberia – yes, there is movement, yes, do not look back. Change itself means birth, movement itself is potential. In this most fundamental sense there is this shared optimism among all readers, a faith in the lines and vectors of the book itself: their forces to propel. And precisely because someplace new is reached, something different is generated the logic of reading necessarily proliferates into a series of temporal differences as well: There is a time to speak and a time to stay silent; there is a time to give and a time to accumulate or acquire. The difference that reading makes, makes time itself divisible. Not everything is right at any time – respect the time for change as much as the time for sharing.

HOW MANY BITS?

It seems that we have stated nothing but the obvious: Reading makes a difference. Reading makes the reader change. And yet, what appears self-evident and utterly indisputable is, as we have seen, not an ahistorical, objective truth but a temporal and alterable idea based on so many hopes, fears, and beliefs and thus susceptible to all kinds of changes. One must therefore also take seriously the possibility that the essential *difference itself* may undergo new and unforeseen transformations in the future, that it may hide and become invisible or that it may one day even completely disappear. In that case there would be nothing preposterous or nonsensical in reaching the very opposite conclusion: "Reading changes nothing. It makes no difference. It leaves me utterly indifferent." What would then be the purpose of reading? Who would be able to explain it? Left only with sacrifices but no gains, restricting and disciplining the body for no apparent reason, reading would seem to be a purely ritualistic and utterly futile practice. Something that previous generations used to do, used to believe in, but which would have lost all relevance and justification since. In fact, there would be so many good reasons *not* to read: All the time spent with a book, all the hours wasted on sitting still: Who can afford it? Who does not have something better and more productive to do? Who does not have other and more important obligations? At best, reading would then appear to be a pastime, a hobby to be practiced whenever there is a bit of free time, whenever all the day's genuine duties and true demands have been met. At worst, it would be the ultimate sign of idleness and of utter purposelessness: A pseudo-activity for society's unintegrated and unassimilated members – the unprogressive, the unadjusted, the unemployed. No one would then be able to save or protect the reader; no arguments would be able to silence the accusations and attacks: You talk of personal growth and progress – but where is the proof? How is it measured? You present yourself as a searcher for truth and a lover of wisdom. But where is the outcome? What have you produced? Faced with such charges the sun kings and adventurers of previous times would be forced to retreat, forced to acknowledge their defeat. Once there is no longer a broad consensus on the benefits of reading, on the difference that it supposedly makes, all arguments in favor grow either hollow or obscure. From the heights of objectivity and truth, from the depths of exploration and intoxication, reading would prove utterly weak and defenseless when brought unto the single plane and narrow frame of simple disbelief. How obvious it would be then that movement is relative to conviction and growth is dependent on persuasion. Where these are missing there is nothing left but empty postulation: A diver brought back on dry land and an escape artist unable to pull off his trick. Without belief none of them budge.

To understand why the practice of reading is today undergoing transformations that threaten to render its purpose highly questionable if not invisible, a new figure and type has to be brought into the investigation and equation: In addition to the diver and the escape artist, one will have

Anders Kølle

to consider carefully the importance of the engineer. At first glance, it would seem that the engineer is thoroughly misplaced in this company – such a strange addition to the history of literature and reading that the thought itself is comical: The man of machines, the inventor and designer of engines, the *homo faber* of apparatuses – who could be further from the spirit of Shakespeare or the poetics of Petrarch? What does the construction of a water pump or the blueprint of a solar panel have in common with a dithyramb or a hexameter? Hasn't Aristotle already separated these spheres and kept theory, practice, and poetics apart? And yet, the engineer is not a delimiting type – he does not abide by the rules and borders imposed from outside. His best work, his proudest machines, are precisely transgressive machines and machines of perpetual trespassing: Engines that produce far more than a single, foreseeable product and serve more than one, unilateral function. Less than conditioned and determined mechanics such machines are veritable catalysts of change – of shock even: The advent of the steam engine – more an event than an invention, more an unleashed power than a contained and canned force. Or the trembling of the telegraph and the light bulb, the telephone and the radio: Who or what remains unaffected? Who does not feel their transformative powers? Their transgressive forces? Autonomous fields and discrete spheres and disciplines suddenly find a common ground and denominator in their equal capacity to be quickly and radically altered: The face of commerce and arts which both look different and for a moment bewildered when exposed to the harsh light of electricity. The sound of music and of politics which is no longer the same when caught on the phonograph or transmitted through the radio. The best engineers are not inventors of singular machines or circumscribable objects – they are inventors of effects and new distributions and assemblages of power far surpassing what their individual ingenuity and intentions can foresee or explain: What they shape is beyond their own imagination and control: A new set of possibilities as well as limitations with the capacity to alter the very way we perceive ourselves as well as each other. Is it any wonder then that the engineer should also have had his effect on the world of literature and books? And that the very doors opened by Gutenberg's printing press or by Hansen's Writing Ball would later be closed by others? That the practice of reading itself turns out to be as vulnerable and perishable as any other human activity or behavior? As we have tried to demonstrate, reading cannot be understood outside the relations that made literature significant to begin with: The relation between man and nature, man and knowledge, man and progress, man and death. Tied to specific hopes and aspirations, particular concepts and ideals, special anxieties and beliefs, reading is only meaningful and desirable as long as these relations and ties remain essentially unbroken. At the beginning of the 21st century, it should, however, be clear that the still recent and revolutionary developments in the world of technology and communication have fundamentally disturbed and irreversibly interrupted the relations and dynamics on which literature and reading hinged. Not that man's fears or beliefs have altogether vanished due to novel machines and inventions. But they have been so thoroughly displaced and pushed in a new direction that the old answers and dreams no longer apply. Beyond the intentions of any single engineer, their work has in effect brought the human species unto a new stage and into a different drama where the man of letters must find himself without a role. Whether this expresses a new zenith of metaphysics and humanism taken to the extreme or whether we should regard this as a sign of the increasing dismantling of human mastery and transcendental subjectivity is a question that can hardly be answered unhesitatingly and unambiguously. In a certain sense, the crisis of literature leads us in both directions and towards both answers at once. Or rather: it leads us into the very mesh and parade of paradoxes that characterize this age and its all-too-human as well as superhuman strivings: How man celebrates himself and his gifts by becoming increasingly inadequate and obsolete – the dream and glory of absolute idleness and unnecessity – yet also a vision permeated with self-suspicion, self-degradation, and self-contempt! How man turns himself into a grand conqueror whose very victories and powers he must both distrust and fear – an army general with nothing left to accomplish but his own, uncompromising defeat! Fabrication of degeneration and impairment, production of self-loathing and self-fear go hand in hand with the unscrupulous narcissism and unlimited self-importance that characterize the spirit of our time.

Some new ideas arrived bombastically and boisterously; almost too sure of themselves – others arrived scarcely noticed, "on doves feet", far from any public attention and any immediate acclaim. Among the former were Wiener's cybernetics and closed signaling and feedback loops. As if everyone had waited impatiently to learn that their own minds were nothing but a circular system and self-governed automaton, Wiener's theories were embraced before they had been actually proved: The demand for genuine verification seemed almost pedantic when the idea itself was so splendid and enticing: Everything is a machine and everyone is a captain on his own machine. There is a bird-captain governing and steering every bird-machine as well as there is a rat-captain, a horse-captain and corresponding rat- and horse-machines. The human mind itself may be a particularly intricate and complex piece of mechanics but isn't it obvious that it too must be a perfectly circular and self-regulatory system abiding by the pure and unquestionable laws of physics and mathematics? Who would not wish to surrender to such a vision? To find the image of himself and his flawed and fallible mind framed by the exact and rigorous language of mathematics? To bathe at least a bit in the bright and serene light of the pure sciences? Wiener himself was surprised and even troubled by this immediate success – his own work and experiments were simply unable to keep pace with public acclaim and imagination. Hence the very reverse problem of what Freud had encountered half a century before: No one rushed to identify with his troubled and muddled model of the mind: Too many labyrinths and too little certainty, too much mummy and daddy and too little stability and predictability. In the choice between being likened to an automaton

Anders Kølle

or a servant of the libido, between being mechanized or psychoanalyzed, there was no doubt what the public preferred and desired the most: The glossy, efficient and tireless machine was infinitely more seductive.

It was, however, the seemingly less sweeping and certainly less exposed ideas and work of others which would turn out to conquer the greatest territory and have the greatest long-term effect: The necessarily secretive work of Alan Turing and his code-breaking apparatus, the electromechanical Bombe – well-hidden and safe from all public attention and scrutiny at Bletchley Park in the English country-side. And although his articles were in principle available to all, could in theory be accessed by anyone, who read his work on computable numbers and the *Entscheidungsproblem*, who could comprehend the implications and importance but a small, select group of his closest peers? Invariant tables of input-output functions, infinite tapes of memory, machines simulating the behavior of other machines – surely there was little in these concepts and in this terminology to spur the interest and the imagination of the many. And so the very basis of the modern day computer, the foundation of our journey into the world of ubiquitous digitization, was laid without the glee, cheer and applause of the crowd: The rotating drums of the Turing-bombe circulated for a long time in public silence.

However influential and truly upending the scientific and engineering breakthroughs of Turing have proven to be on human self-conception, on patterns of work and behavior, on economic as well as cultural production, it is in the work of an even less celebrated mathematician and engineer that our specific inquiry into the history of reading and our analysis of its crisis must take us. A few years after Turing's first discoveries and articles, another paper was published with the hardly sensational or thrilling title "A Mathematical Theory of Communication". On the surface everything seemed absolutely esoteric and perfectly inconsequential and boring for all non-engineers: The author, Claude E. Shannon, was proposing a way to measure amounts of information. Based on this method of measurement he would then proceed with problems of transmission and other calculations: What is the capacity of a communicational channel? How is it decided? And what consequences does this have for the process of encoding? For the accuracy of transmission? For questions of redundancy and noise? Except for the few people who knew that none of these problems had been successfully addressed and solved before, there was not much to find or embrace for anybody else: As long as the radio and the telephone worked, who really cared how? Not the signals and the channels, not the amounts or the bits of information but the *content* was what truly mattered – what was said and meant, not how it was transmitted. And yet, it was precisely this idea that Shannon fundamentally challenged. As he stated unambiguously at the very beginning of his paper: "The fundamental problem of communication is that of reproducing at one point either exactly or approximately a message selected at another point."[2] If the deep secrets of language and communication had puzzled linguists and philosophers,

Anders Kølle

novelists and poets for centuries, Shannon's approach and findings suddenly made all of it look extraordinarily simple: No need to enter into the intricate and labyrinthine theories of a Herder or a Hamann. No need to treat understanding as a complicated art form of stylistic, grammatical, and psychological dimensions. All the paradoxes of the hermeneutic circle and all the complexities of human experience and expression – none of them mattered from Shannon's new perspective, none of them were of significance to his information theory. As the influential mathematician and science consultant Warren Weaver stated in his introduction with a feeling of both victory and relief: "The word *information*, in this theory, is used in a special sense that must not be confused with its ordinary usage. In particular, *information* must not be confused with meaning. In fact, two messages, one of which is heavily loaded with meaning and the other of which is pure nonsense, can be exactly equivalent, from the present viewpoint, as regards information."[3] Finally, unbiased physics and objective mathematics were ready to bring some order into this slippery and emotionally charged domain – ready to take the steering wheel from the shaky and uncertain hands of the humanities: "Say all the nonsense you would like! Be as absurd and superficial or as profound and esoteric as you want. To us, the engineers, it makes no difference. The math remains the same." Due to the invariable operations of binary logarithms – every unit of information being the product of a two-choice situation – it was not only possible to compare and determine the equivalence between two written or spoken messages; between a grocery list and a poem, a political speech and a joke. In fact, it didn't even matter if the messages and symbols were spoken or written, painted or sung, photographed, tapped, clicked, whistled or filmed – the new Shannon theorem applied indiscriminately to them all. If it was possible to express, it was now also possible to measure, calculate and transmit. Hence the supreme universality and triumphant univocality of the theorem: Translated into simple choices, distilled into elementary decisions between "on" or "off", 1 or 0, open or closed, heads or tails, all messages were brought into a common frame, all expressions finally equal before the mathematical law. Similar to the generality of capital exchange relations and to the parallelization of products in the name of the market prize, one was now able to ask: How many bits for a brochure or a bible? What would you like, Sir? A symphony or an instruction book? A small painting or a large cartoon? If you take the cartoon we can also throw in a crossword and a poem! The theorem treated everything evenhandedly – no irrelevant sentimental or snobbish distinctions and discriminations were involved. Wasn't it therefore an age- old egalitarian dream that had come true? Almost a democratic liberation of sorts? For Weaver, at least, the information theory was not simply an effective and omnipotent tool but also an elevated and beautiful ideal: "An engineering communication theory is just like a very proper and discreet girl accepting your telegram. She pays no attention to the meaning, whether it be sad, or joyous, or embarrassing. But she must be prepared to deal with all that come to her desk. This idea that a communication system ought to try to deal with all possible messages, and that the intelligent way to try is to base design on the statistical character of the source, is surely not without significance for communication in general. Language must be designed (or developed) with a view to the totality of things that man may wish to say; but not being able to accomplish everything, it too should do as well as possible as often as possible. That is to say, it too should deal with its task statistically."[4] Whereas the theory itself was now personified as a "very proper, prepared, discreet and acceptant girl", the author, the speaker, the writer, the painter, the poet were collectively depersonalized as "the source". Or to put it in Barthesian terms: the birth of the willing girl was ransomed by the death of the author. But this seeming fancy or phantasm of Weaver was not meant as a simple metaphor. Nor was it only the author who was annihilated in the process. The listener, the reader, the spectator, the audience, the beholder suffered an equal blow: In Shannon's diagram of a general communication system there was only room for a "destination", which described nothing but the necessary and uninteresting terminus, harbor or endpoint of the journey. Clearly, everything truly essential and exciting – the very core of the communication problem, the very thrill of the adventure – was no longer on the side of the author or the reader but only in the calculable activity and transmissions between the two. Hence the redistribution and reversal of life and death: The animation and agency of the channel and the transmitter and the mortification and objectification of the addresser and the addressee.

Questions of progression, development and change were accordingly redirected and concerned now only the system of communication and the flow of information: Not the change or the growth of the reader but the enhancement and optimization of the channel. Not the learning process and knowledge acquisition of the interpreter but the increased rate and efficiency of the coding process. To repeat Shannon's unambiguous maxim: "The fundamental problem of communication is that of reproducing at one point exactly or approximately a message selected at another point." Accuracy and efficiency thus supplanted understanding and creativity. If one could not count on the source and the destination to stand still, to remain fixed, unaffected and essentially unprogressive, the entire calculus would fall apart! There would be no math or method of measuring able to deal with change and growth in every direction. Just as the message had to be separated from meaning so the destination had to be separated from movement. The risky and indeterminate reader was henceforth effaced not only from the vocabulary but also in effect: As a bulwark against the undesirable impact of human agency and interpretation a device or extra "station" was interposed between the signal and the destination and thus before the message reached its end. The function of this station, the receiver, was none other than to perform the inverse operation of that done by the transmitter and hence to reconstruct or decode what had been encrypted or encoded at the beginning of the trajectory. Surely, everyone could agree on the receiver's necessity: From electrical currents on the telephone wire to electromagnetic waves traveling through air, some intermediary was needed which would provide the translation and produce comprehensible words and images out of unfathomable signals and inhuman noise. In the electronic age, without the job of the receiver, one man stood utterly helpless before another man's distant utterance and intent. The true place of magic and mindboggling transformation lay therefore in the performance of this hidden and potent device: Where there were buzz and vibration there suddenly came voice. Where there were nothing but invisible waves there came image and sound. To laymen this was miraculous and surreal. To Shannon and his peers this was simple and controlled engineering. But it had the much desired and important effect of taking the uncertain work of the reader out of the loop and releasing the human interpreter of all duties: To be reducible and containable as a *point* at the very end of the process, all the significant tasks had to be performed *before* reaching this point. It had to be plausible and thereby calculable that the destination did nothing but pick up and receive. That *in* the end and *as* the end, he was simply a landing spot for the message – essentially no different from a coat stand or a shoe rack: A convenient place to store or "hang" the signal. And surely Shannon's diagram did give him little else to do: Instead of deciphering the hieroglyphs of existence, the reader was handed the decoded information of the system; instead of embarking on a journey into the great unknown, the interpreter was supposed patiently to await the ringing of the phone. The less he reached for anything, the less he questioned or challenged the process, the less he intervened or sought transformation and growth, the more perfectly did he fit into Shannon's neat diagram. Of course the art of immobilization was hardly a new discipline for the reader. Centuries of practice had made him a master of this particular art form. But whereas the reading of books had demanded the sacrifice of the body in order to liberate and elevate the spirit, it was in Shannon's diagram almost the other way around: The body and flesh could be as free as it wanted, move around as much and frenetically as it liked, as long as the mind restricted itself to the role of destination and the confines of the endpoint. The calculability of the transmission and the efficiency of the system demanded this sacrifice. And who didn't want communication to happen smoothly? Who wouldn't want faster and still more information? An immaculate, untainted flow? In fact, there were even reasons to begin to wonder whether humans were needed in the process at all? If it might not be better altogether, more efficient, to cut them out entirely? Shannon for one clearly saw the potential and began discreetly to play with the idea. Here is how he briefly and densely defined the very end of the communication line: "The *destination* is the person (or thing) for whom the message is intended."[5] No doubt he would rather have put *person* than *thing* in parentheses. But now at least the idea was introduced: Communication did not need to be between humans. It was entirely possible – and undoubtedly better from an engineering perspective, yes, better for communication itself – if man was erased once and for all. His very presence, even if only at the very beginning and end, always posed the risk

Anders Kølle

of failure, of somehow interfering, intermingling and fucking it up. The very evolution of communication was at stake! Its very future! Wasn't it then, in fact, petty of man to stand in the way? Selfish even? Nothing but good old stubbornness and pride! There were already enough problems with thermal and electromagnetic noise as it were. Why also add psychological and semantic noise? The special human susceptibility to error: to going awry and being led astray – to misunderstand and miscalculate, to misjudge and misbehave. And so, in the very name of communication, for the very sake of communication – please, do keep man away!

INFORMATION, REFORMATION, TRANSFORMATION

Today the importance of Shannon's theorem and discoveries is undisputed among experts and engineers: What would information theory have been without them? For how long would man have continued to complicate life for himself and fumble in the dark without grasping the essence and building blocks of communication? If not for Shannon, how impatiently would we not have waited for someone to enlighten us and show us the way? Here is an ode in Shannon's honor by two contemporary professors of computer engineering, Bruce Hajek and Richard E. Blahut: "The fact that a specific capacity can be reached, and that no data transmission system can exceed this capacity, has been the holy grail of modem design for the last fifty years. Without the guidance of Shannon's capacity formula, modem designers would have stumbled more often and proceeded more slowly. Communication systems ranging from deep-space satellite links to storage devices such as magnetic tapes and ubiquitous compact disks, and from high-speed internets to broadcast high-definition television, came sooner and in better form because of his work. Aside from this wealth of consequences, the wisdom of Claude Shannon's insights may in the end be his greatest legacy."[6] Reading the two professors' commemoration, one is reminded of the deep affection Weaver always had for *Alice's Adventures in Wonderland*: It is as if Shannon's channel was in fact a magic rabbit hole leading to a most extraordinary and enchanted new world of technological opportunities – as if his findings energized, animated, even spirited the entire world of communication systems to the point that ubiquitous compact disks and high-speed internet came dancing from the future: A very real wonderland of high-definition television, magnetic tapes, and deep-space satellites. It all came alive, it all came true – at least sooner – because of Shannon. And yet, all that aside, or in addition, seemingly reaching the two professors from a different channel and on a different frequency, *"it is the wisdom of Claude Shannon's insights"* that *"may in the end be his greatest legacy."* And so ends also the ode and commemoration. Certainly not without a feeling of both tension and suspense: Wouldn't one like to know what these insights and this wisdom were? Why not say a word about them? Why leave the most essential part of Shannon's legacy in silence? As something unnamable and ineffable. Or worse: as something incalculable and incomputable. Is it possible that Shannon's true legacy is simply too large to transmit? Or too difficult to reduce to a binary choice? A flip-flop-situation?

One aspect of Shannon's legacy that is certainly hard to quantify and possibly unlikely for most engineers to appreciate and fully recognize, is the effect his theory and thoughts have had far from the closed orbits of deep-space satellites and well beyond the scope of information theory itself. As with the invention of the steam engine or the electric light, Shannon's theorem set new powers in motion producing new distributions and assemblages of forces, energies and effects. Something became obvious which had

Anders Kølle

previously been hidden – and something else retreated into the electric shadows and was forgotten in the old and soon obsolete noisy channels. To our specific inquiry into the practice and history of reading it is obvious how the turn towards information theory and the new axioms of communication from the very outset, in their very essence, challenged the movement and difference, the journey and advancement on which the value of reading hinged. Whether one regards it from the perspective of escape and transcendence or from the viewpoint of growth and intoxication – whether the reader's primary identification is with the escape artist or with the diver, with the hero of heights or the explorer of depths – the grand information revolution has had dire consequences. And how could it be any different when all the proudest ideals of literature, its tallest spires and deepest and most secret chambers, its grandest hopes and most mysterious aspirations, have found themselves transported onto new ground, into a new light, under a new law and logic, where they encounter so little interest and such scarce appreciation? Where the significance of interpretation is minimized while the importance of information flow is maximized? Where the distinction between meaning and nonsense is leveled out, while the difference between slow and fast has become paramount? Where priority is no longer given to the secluded contemplator but to the connected communicator – no longer to the lonely traveler but to the prolific chatterer? Core literary values which used to be self-evident are therefore far from indisputable anymore: The significance of silent contemplation as a means to change, to grow, to rise, to see. The faith in the inner journey and the solitary ascent or dive: The man who distances himself, still further up, out, or down, still further away. Not out of disregard or contempt for his fellow men, not out of any misplaced anger or spite, but because he believes that some journeys cannot be shared, that some insights and secrets, some knowledge and wisdom, speak only to the man who approaches them alone. Hence the necessarily asocial appearance of the reader, the unapproachable man with his book. Where is he going? What is he becoming? What is he metamorphosing into? In silence he changes, in stillness he moves and grows. Yet, he cares little about sharing, yet, he cares little for speaking or transmitting, sending or communicating. For now it is not adequacy but difference, not equality but distinction, not reproduction but creation that interests him. How, therefore, could he be an endpoint or a destination – he who is constantly evolving and on the way? And how could he be a source of information – he who is still only a student and an apprentice and doesn't yet have something to say? Thus the strange and intermediary space of the reader: the space of contemplation, interpretation, and transformation which the age of information finds it so hard to understand and accommodate.

From the growth of the individual to the growth of data and information, from the development of the reader to the progress of the means and channels of communication: Along these lines of displacement leading to new centers of attention, the fears and anxieties of people are changing too. If it was the noise of worldly contingency which

Anders Kølle

frightened the escape artist and the end of progress and enchantment which scared the diver, it is now silence which scares the chatterer and communicator. For the stronger and faster the flow of data and communication has become, the harder it is for silence be interpreted in more than one single way: As a screaming testimony to one's utter insignificance, one's total negligibility. To wake up to an empty mail-box or go to bed with no new messages on the phone: Is my existence really so irrelevant? Am I truly all alone? Since all vitality, dynamicity, and importance have been allocated to the channels and the tubes, to the continuous flows and transmissions, being cut off or finding oneself on the outside means that one seems far from the very source of life itself: Like a leaf fallen from the tree or a flower cut off from the stem – can the severed or disconnected do anything but slowly wither and grow pale, weak, and sick? In the Age of Information silence is therefore necessarily alarming. Or to be more exact: Silence is precisely *not silent*, for it signifies and exhibits a distance and a gap which is no longer desirable but only terrifying. To look into this gap thus means two very different, even opposite, things for the reader of previous times and the communicator of today: Whereas the former found liberating potential in the very absence of sound and distraction – as if silence was a shelter or a greenhouse for new inspirations, insights, and ideas – the latter sees only failure in the absence, finds only menace in the gap. What silence now says is therefore no longer: "Use me and sculpt me! Turn me into something magnificent and new!" But: "Avoid me, escape me, flee from me if you can.

Because once we are together it means that you are on your own." Hence the migration away from all lonely and isolated places, from any secluded and peripheral heights or depths and into the network of communication, still closer to the tubes, channels and pulse of information. And so, in this new age, the phone and the computer, the TV and the radio, are not only simple media or means of transmission but rather genuine safeguards and friends: Like watchdogs they protect their owner and keep the danger of absence and silence away. One can feel safe in their company, one can trust them to be constantly ready and alert: Every time the gap seems to be increasing or stillness is lurking in the night, the media and the technologies never fail to remove the danger in a swoop: A football match on the radio or a talk show on TV, a documentary about the Second World War or a tweet from a celebrity. Does it really matter which? Should it? Isn't the only essential thing to be close to the flow and remain inside the network? If so, one would inevitably have to concede that Shannon was right from the very start: The true problem of communication is not one of meaning or of content but exclusively a question of transmission and reproduction: Send a cooking recipe or a painting, disseminate pure nonsense or grand and visionary ideas – in the world of bits and information they are all treated equally.

With Shannon's theorem we have thus moved away from the questions of height and depth and away from any hierarchical structure based on individual development and growth: The silent scholar and the man of letters are

Anders Kølle

increasingly seen as pitiful rather than heroic figures: Have they not understood that the world has changed? That they are playing an old and outdated game? That no one fears the enemies they are fighting and no one celebrates the victories they win? There is a woman who has studied Balzac for ten years. She is now an expert on his authorship. Who would like to hear about it? There is a man who has just finished a lengthy book on the thinking of Aristotle. Who will buy it and read it? Who has the time? Yesterday's experts and masters look more and more like fools in today's world: First they disappear for too long and then they return with too much to say. Or, which amounts to the same: First they underestimate the *im*patience of others and then they overestimate their patience. Like ballroom dancers at a rave party it may be hard to tell whether they are one step ahead or one step behind – but surely they are continuously out of sync. This testifies to the growing importance that rhythm and frequency attain as communication itself is increasingly emptied of specific content and meaning: It would seem that the less the individual messages actually *say*, the more significant it becomes to repeat nothing all the time. A new order has emerged in which the sheer rate of transmissions and signals comes to play the main role and appears purposeful in itself. Hence the pressure that is now felt to continuously state, report, announce, or release something new: What matters is not if it is rich, moving or profound – only that it happens often: The pulse of communication supersedes the quality of exchanges. And so, in both public and private life, a sense of urgency and necessity is introduced to perpetually broadcast and disseminate, update and promulgate: The times are past when the university professor could ponder on the same questions for years and years before putting anything into writing. If she wants to remain relevant – if she wants to stay employed – she cannot hesitate and contemplate for too long but must constantly publish and present her theories and findings – often, therefore, before any new findings or discoveries have been made: For indeed: Who has the time to wait? The longer the list of publications, the more frequently her name appears in journals and in research papers, the higher her esteem. Similar conditioned are today's doctors, nurses, lawyers, and policemen: Still less time is spent with the patients, the clients, the victims and still more with registering and monitoring and sending data back and forth. The channels of communication demand constant nurturing and attention, asking to be fed again and again. A century ago the following message from Proust counted as a strange but amusing joke: "My dear Madame, I just noticed that I forgot my cane at your house yesterday; please be good enough to give it to the bearer of this letter. P.S. Kindly pardon me for disturbing you; I just found my cane." But what was still humorous prior to the invention of the internet and the smartphone has become commonplace and expected since: Asking for attention for no apparent reason is the norm rather than the exception in the insatiable worlds of Facebook, Twitter, Instagram: Here is a picture of the sandwich I just ate – "notice that the crust was a little dry" – and there is a new text message on my phone: "Please bring my raincoat to the picnic! Oh, but now the rain has already stopped. By the way, I can't come to the picnic."

Anders Kølle

However, it is not only a lack of irony which separates today's exchanges from Proust's letter. More importantly, it is a lack of confidence and certitude: To the extent that the very condition of appreciation, the very possibility of appearing relevant and valuable has become inseparable from the channels and flows of communication, from the beats and pulse of information, one cannot but feel helplessly lost without them. To be inside or outside, to be connected or not, to be "on" or "off" – along this thin and constantly moving fault line entire careers, friendships and stories of love seem to be decided. It would therefore be a grave mistake to consider all the meaninglessness and trivia distributed through the computer and the phone as precisely *insignificant*: From an existential perspective they have in fact become quintessential. Only by constantly probing the net, ceaselessly testing the flow does one gain a sense of reality and of genuine existence. But this sense is always ephemeral, cannot but be brief and insubstantial. For where will the flow move to next? Who will it grace and invigorate in a moment with its vital streams? And what are the chances that I will be remembered? That I will still be cared about and loved? Hence every text message and update functions like the ceaselessly testing and moving tip of a blind person's cane: It is a means to measure and scan one's surroundings – to estimate one's current position as one tries to navigate and move forward in the unpredictable and ever-changing landscape of the net.

Now, when regarded from this new perspective – communication as orientation – it becomes clear why lengthy and semantically complex messages are not only unnecessary but even undesirable and potentially detrimental: When the primary aim is immediate and unambiguous feedback, the updates made and the text messages send forth must be equally univocal and easy for everyone to instantly discern and decipher. Shannon's concern with the "human noise factor", man's innate inclination to complicate matters and slow processes down, has to some extent proven unnecessary: People themselves constantly seek to simplify their language and expressions and to censor ambiguities and cut any polysemousness off. Hence the general eradication of foreign or challenging word constellations and the collective turn towards the shortest and most elementary linguistic components: Only sentences that fit within the frame of common understanding and conform to the schema of univocal communication are allowed unto the Facebook wall or into the Twitter account. Inevitably the very possibility of expressing any kind of nuances or promulgating any sense of uncertainty or hesitation is thereby precluded. That is: thoughts and emotions, sensations and experiences must equally conform to the narrow frame of greatly diminished options that a highly standardized and increasingly amputated language provides. And so the desire to express a subtle feeling or communicate an indeterminate thought or sensation is constantly overshadowed and pushed aside by what has become the predominant purpose of texting and messaging: To re-measure and re-orient oneself vis-à-vis the constant stream of information. The question *where* one stands in regard to the value and vitality given by the flow thus supersedes the desire for more genuine exchanges and greater liberty of expression. Only the plain, short message serves the purpose of localization well: a message that like sonar probes the virtual "waters" and reveals one's position and current distance or proximity to one's network, contacts, family, and friends. How quickly is the message returned – how fast do the "sound waves" or signal bounce back? Or how many "likes" and how fast the response? From this an immediate estimation of one's current situation in terms of relevance, popularity, esteem, and love is made.

With this background it should not be surprising to find that the logic and the dominance of probing and testing and the resultant abbreviations, standardizations, and simplifications come to set their mark on culture as a whole: In order to receive immediate feedback and unambiguous data and information, nuances and semantic complexity are increasingly shunned due to the muddled and belated response they all too easily produce. Everything must be made simple and short so it fits the schema and frame of indubitable communication and provides a clear picture of the current situation: Surely, it is no coincidence that it was first the black master of Facebook and then the white king of Twitter who made it to the oval office in the USA. But it is not only political ideas and messages which are trimmed and tailored to meet the new standards. Even in domains traditionally characterized by emotional richness and complexity, by semantic density and multifacetedness, the razor of abbreviations and simplifications is threating to cut all intricacies off: Today's filmmakers and composers, singers and actors appear no less than politicians preoccupied with standardizing their expressions and ideas in order to fit their work into the novel paradigm of swift and one-dimensional communication: Every depicted emotion and sensation, every narrative or musical motif and phrasing, seems, almost in advance, afraid of challenging or transgressing against the narrow boundaries of immediate recognition and unhesitant identification: The face of anger, rage and revenge that some actors have made it their specialty and entire career to endlessly render and repeat; the sound of melancholy and heartache that can only be instrumentalized and phrased in one particular way. Joy is always upbeat and sadness is always slow. Even before the actor or singer delivers the first line or note the entire spectrum of expressive possibilities and endless field of semantic constellations have already been sacrificed for the sake of absolute transparency and unconditional poignancy: The eyes of the singer are closed, both hands are clutching the microphone, she looks alone on the stage – abandoned in the spotlight: How deep are not her emotions? How sad does she not appear? Who can doubt for a second what the song is meant to make us feel? Affect and efficiency thus appear coupled from the very outset: Immediate recognition and instantaneous identification render any interpretation superfluous: The message is not revealed through *understanding* but already disclosed and exhausted in the very act of transmitting and announcing. The film contains nothing that its title and poster have not beforehand made clear; the song evokes

Anders Kølle

with precision what the performer seems almost predestined to sense and declare. Or to repeat Shannon's theorem one more time: "The fundamental problem of communication is that of reproducing at one point either exactly or approximately a message selected at another point." Hence the need to make affections reproducible and unmistakable – that is: to transform them into signals which can be channeled with a minimum of interference or noise: A song about love, a film about lust, a play about loss. What exceeds or challenges the simplicity of the message is no longer a sign of artistry but of unprofessionalism: The inability to express oneself in accordance with the schema of one-dimensional communication. A good and potentially successful melodic line is therefore one which never strays too far from its single scope or simple statement and returns repeatedly to the refrain. A good storyline for a movie or a play is unidirectional and can be summed up in one or two sentences or catchphrases: *Now he is back for revenge – this time he takes no prisoners*. Stereotypes and clichés, samplings, references and reuse only facilitate the cultural reproduction and serve the translation of emotion and expression into signal and information. The goal is instant appreciation and indiscriminate accessibility. Hence the charts and billboards are filled with singles that sound perfectly familiar: *Love Me Now, Don't Let Me Down, Think A Little Less, Party Monster, Water Under The Bridge*. No estrangement, schism or alterity is allowed to endanger the communicational clearness and conformity. The real *creative* and *artistic* problem lies in fact less in the transmission than in the *selection* and the *choice* – or what Norbert Wiener terms the *decision*: "One of the simplest, most unitary forms of information is the recording of a choice between two equally probable simple alternatives, one or the other of which is bound to happen – a choice, for example, between heads and tails in the tossing of a coin. We shall call a single choice of this sort a *decision*."[7] On or off, dash or dot, heads or tails: Here is the *kind of decision* that the songwriter and producer must make: Should the next single release be a love song or not? A party track or not? What does the audience, the fans, the public want? Hence the artist and the producer find themselves facing a decision that returns them to the unpredictable and ever changing flows of activity and attention: Only a sort of cultural echolocation is helpful in these turbulent waters: Songs, films, plays that like the repetitive and short clicking sounds and whistles of dolphins and bats make navigation seem possible. To the artist the single release and the movie trailer are therefore primarily of interest for the echo and information they produce: A snapshot of the cultural scene and cultural trends before they transmute and move on. If a song or a movie can still be said to have a touching quality, it is inevitably a new and different touch that the public or audiences feel: Not the touch of a caress or of affection but of a constant search and endless testing: No longer hands that seek to sculpt, grasp or create but only to point, identify and locate. And so, the hands of the artist let go as soon as they find and find only to let go. Every work thus becomes as light and inconsequential as the touch of a blind person: A scanning touch of an attention in constant movement.

Anders Kølle

Nothing is reformed or sought to be altered; nothing is enhanced, strengthened and heightened or lessened, weakened and destroyed – there is only a movement across surfaces, a neglectful and forgetful touch along outlines. The feel of the artist has therefore turned both unfilled and unfulfilling: void of any intention that exceeds the traversing itself or reaches for more than what can immediately be left behind, there is no longer any ambition to form, to hold, and to keep. This lack of investment, of connection, and of commitment is not only what turns the relationship between artist and audience into a hollow postulation but also what constantly disrupts and alienates the relationship between the artist and her work: What is produced is only produced to be abandoned – which is to say: What is created has already been deserted from the beginning: As pure signal and echo, as traveling light waves or sound waves, as cultural "clicks" in the information flow, the artistic message is predestined to disappear. Impermanence and inconsequence preclude any emotional investment or sense of deeper attachment. What is permanent is only a constant letting go: For the sake of continued and future relevance no work can afford to be truly relevant. Or as Bernard Stiegler has recently written: "... *our epoch...* is *distinguished by the fact that imprints are erased as they are produced*, as though the wax in which they are left has heated up so much that it has become liquid and can no longer serve as *solid* matter... This fluidity that no longer retains anything (which is the fluidity of the `fifteen minutes of fame') is retentionally lacking. It is endlessly traversed by a flux of goods, messages, sounds and images that become completely indifferent. Itself a flux, this fluidity becomes indifferent in turn, and nothing, it seems, can happen to it any longer: we have here an *anesthesia, which therefore learns nothing* of the horrifyingly accidental events that never stop taking place and multiplying *at the edges* of the flow of goods, threatening to discharge into it like so many poisons."[8] At the edges of the flow a catastrophe is repeated which never turns stable and solid enough to serve as a lesson. And so the poisons are in fact already discharged: There is nothing to learn or retain from the constant flux of messages, images, and sounds – nothing, perhaps, but the ephemeral non-lesson of inconsequence itself. Hence the great paradox of our epoch: What is strangely missing in the Age of Information is the ability and volition to *in*-form anything. To *in*-form and thus to shape and give form would require a level of commitment and engagement which is incompatible with the traveling attention of constant orientation and the perpetual demands of the flux. As such, *in*-formation would in fact be a gift and a token of attention and appreciation which the urgency of constant communication makes it increasingly difficult to produce and to give. For understood as a gift *in*-formation is not simply a matter of promulgating or disseminating – it cannot be reduced to sheer signals, numbers, and calculations. Instead of statistics and binary choices or simple decisions it would ask of us that we *create*, *invest* and *invent* on a conceptual and emotional terrain that is significantly vaster than the narrow scope and field of common understanding and one-dimensional communication. It would be to open the gates once more to the risk of noise and

Anders Kølle

misunderstandings: In other words: Not to make a choice but to take a chance. The chance that inescapably accompanies any desire to sculpt and call into light: The distortions and deformations that might appear instead of the affirmations; the odd and incomprehensible that suddenly seizes an idea or overpowers a figure. To put uncontrollable and possibly devastating powers into play in order to present you with something, in order to give or pass on. *In-formation's* possibility of genuinely *in*-forming, of being an actual *gift*, would thus necessarily mean to face and confront unpredictable risks. Failure and complete misapprehension would continuously threaten to dissolve or destroy. But *in*-formation would not be a gift despite these risks and despite this threat: Rather it becomes precisely a gift *because* of the dangers that perpetually traverse any coming-into-form; the danger that it already is to want to give someone something. Hence the abyss that separates Wiener's and Shannon's notion of information as choice and decision from a concept of *in*-formation as risk and as gift. Whereas the former will necessarily seek to govern and delimit chance by forcing it into a binary choice and a simple opposition, the latter must set chance free, give chance a chance, in order to *in*-form something of both necessity and significance: Forms with the potential to make a difference and to *trans*-form. This was the sense in which any communicator was originally also a sort of artist – before artists reduced themselves to pure and poor communicators. Or as the sculptor Joseph Beuys once put it: "Already in thought the process of putting into form is established which later, by way of bodily organs and other tools, will appear as imprinted in the world, taking on there a form that informs: information for another being who needs this information in the form of a product, or else considers the information as a message that the other can receive."[9] And further: "The action of man, or his information, his imprinting nature – imprinting something in a form - , should this in-formation be considered in terms of a process proceeding from a free decision, from the freedom of this being? With this imprinting nature we get to the point where we must speak of a sculptural process: imprinting an act in matter. In this act, the sculptor is barely distinguishable from the printer."[10] For readers, writers, literates, and bookworms of previous times there would hardly be anything surprising or striking in the words of Beuys – nothing but truisms and banalities: Of course the speaker or writer is imprinting his thoughts in some kind of matter, and of course he does so for the sake of others: that they may receive it and be informed by it. One gives form in order to in-form those who want it or need it. Why else should one speak or write? Produce and construct sentences and meanings? But, paradoxically, it is not in previous times but in our own time, in the Age of Information itself that the words of Beuys have come to sound increasingly odd – even romantic and naïve: Who can still believe that the ever-increasing amount of information exists somehow for them? Is it for their benefit alone? Does it answer their individual needs or desires? Or, even more incredible: Is it to be regarded as a gift? A genuine offering? It would require an engagement and a risk, a will to form surpassing all uncertainties and all white and semantic noise, which seem increasingly inadequate and even inappropriate

Anders Kølle

in a time of abbreviations, reductions, and expressive limitations. Not to comply with the rules and expectations of short and prefigured, predictable communication might in fact appear onerous instead of generous: The lengthy and semantically rich message which calls for more attention and commitment than one may be willing to receive and return. And yet, we may ask, when the gift and the creation are removed from communication and reduced to a simple decision and a binary choice – what is it in fact that we transmit and receive? What is it that we are constantly sending back and forth? Shannon called it bits and believed that the *mathematical answer* and the *engineering model* would and should suffice. But what he didn't apprehend from his purely practical perspective – or, what he did not feel the *need* to apprehend – was that the moment he called information calculable and meaning irrelevant, his gift to communication was nothing but an annulment of its very raison d'être. Here is Warren Weaver's terribly misguided appraisal of the scientific breakthrough: "This is a theory so general that one does not need to say what kinds of symbols are being considered – whether written letters or words, or musical notes, or spoken words, or symphonic music or pictures. The theory is deep enough so that the relationships it reveals indiscriminately apply to all these and to other forms of communication. This means, of course, that the theory is sufficiently imaginatively motivated so that it is dealing with the real inner core of the communication problem – with those basic relationships which hold in general, no matter what special form the actual case may take."[11] But we should ask: what are these basic relationships? And more importantly: what are relationships which *hold in general*? Have humans ever been in a *general relationship*? Been something to each other *in general*? Expressed, sung, written, said, filmed, painted something *in general* and thus regardless of what "the special form of the actual case may take". And so, the basic question and fundamental problem can be put very simply: Who or what is still *in*-formed when the form itself has turned irrelevant and the relationship become an abstraction? The answer is not hard to find and will only confirm our previous suspicions: What Weaver, like Shannon, has in mind is no longer mankind but calculating, universal machines. Hence the great malaise of *still* being human and attempting to be something for others and express something to others under machinic conditions – in a language void of creation, singularity and gifts. Inevitably – to humans – these conditions bring uncertainty and fear: Deprived of the means to *in*-form our surroundings we are constantly in doubt about our own relevance and relations. We interact and perform as prolific and reliable communication machines but are left alone with our ungeneralizable humanity: Our irreducible singularity which does not conform to the schema of efficient and swift communication. What I think and feel, who I believe to be, is in this sense always too much for the channels I am offered. Not because existence was ever a kind of knowledge. But because existence was *in*-formed by the act of expression. In shaping a message rather than selecting or choosing one, the individual would also give form to herself: That is: The gift of forming and giving was not least a gift to the giver. Hence

Anders Kølle

something was given and something was shared which were the very opposite of a generalization: The particularity and irreducibility of both the addresser and the addressee. As Marcel Proust beautifully put it: "By art alone we are able to get outside ourselves, to know what another sees of this universe which for him is not ours, the landscapes of which would remain as unknown to us as those of the moon."[12] But this is not the task of art alone. Nor are the landscapes steady horizons. Rather Proust describes an act of *in*-formation and a process of communication: To share what isn't shared, what cannot be shared, and is shared precisely as such. The impossibility of sharing is thus indeed shared and miraculously made possible. Isn't this the great marvel of communication? What urges us to take the risks to *in*-form? To take a chance with another? To wish to speak, to write, to sing? If so, we do not engage in communication in order to orientate ourselves or to measure the distance or the proximity, the love and the affection of others. Nor do we speak or write with the purpose of "reproducing a message". The reproduction and representation remain uninteresting, anonymous, and barren if they are not *in*-formed: If it does not create and offer change, if it does not offer the possibility to trans-form and re-form. Hence Shannon's essential misunderstanding and misfortunate reversal: The fundamental problem of communication is not how to make the same but how to offer difference: How to present difference as an opportunity and as a gift. Then reproduction can never be the end or the purpose but only a means, and representation is not a simple repetition but the possibility of a re-form: The sharing through words, images, sounds of the unbridgeable gap which separates us and which we therefore seek and need to give form to: Hence the risk of communication which is always more than a simple, binary choice: For no words are exchanged in which an abyss and a void are not speaking too: To show you, "what I see of this universe which for you is not yours" is necessarily to step onto an edge. And every word and sentence must be formed and sculpted along this edge, presented and offered from this edge. But therein lie not only the vertigo but also the thrill of communication: Because we may fail and fall, we may also revel and rejoice. A message that gets across is a dance on the edge and a testimony to the impossible made possible.

There are therefore important reasons to remember what both Proust and Beuys made quite clear: To communicate is to offer a difference in the form of *in*-formation. And this difference is never generalizable since the risk and the gift are respectively taken and given at the very edge of particularity, of "what I see of this universe which for me is not yours". As we have tried to show, literature and the act of reading always made this difference stand out: Why read if not for the possibility of a re-form? Why read if not to be trans-formed? For the sake of creation and becoming? Words, then, were not meant to reproduce or represent. Nor were they reducible to a simple choice and selection. Instead they were disclosers of an opportunity produced and evoked by the very distance separating the reader from the writer. Hence the reader's need for silence and contemplation:

Anders Kølle

Always much too easy and tempting to make same, to see and hear nothing but an echo and a repetition, it requires great concentration and determination to keep the difference alive and thereby to be susceptible to the gift that the text and its author has to offer. That is why inter-pretation cannot simply be bypassed or taken out of the equation, such as Shannon prompted us to do. And that is why the information source and destination cannot be faithfully represented as immoveable "points". For just as points have no edges nor expansion and therefore no potential for reform – so communication without inter-pretation annuls the very distance and difference that makes sharing into a gift. But it should come as no surprise that Shannon was never keen to look down into this void. Had he done so it would have been impossible for him to generalize communication and mathematize in-formation. And he would have made no progress in clearing the way for the eventual takeover of the machines. All he would have seen would have been thoroughly disappointing – human, all-too-human – something for humanists and romantics more than for engineers: how humans try to reach for each other, how they try to share something unshareable between them.

But we must still ask: If the Age of Information is not truly deserving of its name – at least from a human perspective – and if communication no longer means precisely sharing – then, what is it that is distributed and transmitted like never before? What is it that we constantly disseminate and receive? Surely, we already know what others have taught us to call it, the names that have been hijacked in order to keep the public excited and aboard. Here is the promise: "Connectivity like never before. Everything accessible, everybody close." And for those who were already excited about Wiener's cybernetics and about the prospect of being as wonderful, reliable, productive, loveable, and sexy as a machine: "Yes, you too may become an automaton and a chatterbox that never stops. Always on and never off the future belongs to you." And yet, despite the attempt of social media to generalize human relations and despite the enthusiasm with which new channels of communication are instantly embraced, there remains *something* which is not quite up to speed, *something* which cannot quite adapt: *Something*, therefore, which is the cause of embarrassment or even shame and which is rarely said out loud but often whispered in the night: "Despite everything, I am still lonely..." How truly mysterious and odd to feel this way in the Age of Information and of constant communication! How strangely inappropriate! But nevertheless the feeling may not be easy to shake, may not seem to answer to common sense and sound reason. And the more the feeling of loneliness is despised and sought to be forgotten and pushed aside, the stronger does it seem to color and permeate every word and conversation: Suddenly it is all I read in the text message and all I hear in someone's voice. Soon it is all that confronts me in the movie theater and all I encounter in a song. Everywhere the same solitude and everything just its tired mirror. But however redundant and repetitive, however foreseeable and tiresome in the end, these endless repetitions can offer no appeasement or consolation because what is repeated is

Anders Kølle

constantly my exclusion: "Not only are you alone – but you are also alone *being alone*, your loneliness is shared by no one." Isolated in the midst of communication I can therefore only blame myself, blame my singularity and particularity which appear to continuously stand in the way. What I want and need to share the most seems therefore to be precisely what makes the sharing itself impossible. However eagerly I may attempt to subdue and repress my singularity, it always returns to haunt every attempt and act of communication: I come to stand out where I must hope to disappear; I come to see only myself where I most want to retreat or completely vanish. Which also means: the distance and difference between me and others appear as an unsolvable problem and as a constant cause of unrest. At once a hole in the spoken and something that overflows any speech, it becomes both a lack in the said and what exceeds all expression. It is too much – it is too little, which is to say: It is permanently disruptive and unsettling. Hence the communicative surplus which *is also a deficit*: What makes me fall short and yet be too much in and for every act of communication. The unshareable itself which constantly blocks yet requires more communication. And so the sense of loneliness only grows the more I communicate, the more I send back and forth. Every message being nothing but a hollow echo of the same hopeless hope and impossibility of mutuality: Signals of a lacking touch and of an irreducible distance – signals which must perpetually reach out and come back – only to be sent on their way once more. I cannot escape myself – and it is precisely this that seems to me to be the painful problem. If only there were words in which I could vanish, if only there were messages into which I could dissolve. Then nothing would stand between me and others since I would become one with the communicative flow: Everywhere and nowhere instead of alone in my irreplaceable here and now; indistinguishable and indifferent instead of different and in despair. Hence I try to give my difference away: Not as a gift but as a secret, not as a source of value but as a reason for embarrassment and shame. What I see of this universe which for you is not yours, is precisely what I do not want to see anymore – and what I expect no one would be interested in seeing. And so I teach myself to step into commonness, to dress my thoughts in indistinct and inconspicuous phrases. I find in immediacy and shallowness a shelter, and in linguistic abbreviations and standardizations a friend. I learn to respond quickly, without hesitation – to simply react instead of reflect. I discipline my penchant for nuances and graduations and trim all intricacies and double meanings off. In a language thus cleansed of particularity and originality but rich in indifference and anonymity, I reach for the general as the place of final deliverance and ultimate sharing: Here where no one is something to someone, all are united in being nothing for all. Haven't we now solved the riddle awaiting us at the very core of the communication problem? What Shannon and Weaver already brought into a theorem and presented as a communication law? If meaning is taken out of the message and accurate reproduction replaces creation, interpretation, and transformation, and if information is independent of form and particularity and relations are generalized into numbers and abstractions –

Anders Kølle

then, indeed, the communication problem would seem to have been solved. Thus clarity and calculability supplant singularity and semantic noise just as binary choices and simple decisions replace the chances and risks of giving distance and difference a particular form. Then I need no longer consider what I see of this universe which is mine and not yours, for only indifference stands between us in a single universe already shared by all. And yet, doesn't some doubt remain? Some uncertainty hidden beneath or between the bits and the meaningless messages? Will I ever have succeeded in burying or giving my difference completely away? Or will it once more come back to haunt me and separate and isolate me from the communication flow? Suspended between the singular and the general I would thus once more encounter my irreducible, unplaceable humanity.

THE TECHNOLOGICAL SUBLIME

And so my loneliness will return, it must return: For it is inevitably present in the doubts that never fail to come back to me and in the fear that never grows tired of tormenting me: When will my hideout be discovered and my forgery be exposed? When will indifference no longer cover and harbor me but difference once more single me out? Force me to make this ridiculous, sad confession: "Yes, I must admit, I was never one of you. I was never one *with* you. I only pretended for a while." And the verdict? The punishment? Everyone's complete indifference – which means: Solitary confinement for life. Hence the new kind of loneliness, the new face of solitude that the age of communication produces: No longer a shared, human condition, no longer an inborn, existential dilemma, it appears instead as an extraordinarily cruel exception – and as individual failure and inaptitude. And as the possibilities for contemplation and interpretation are increasingly obfuscated by endless communication itself, the *means* to address and understand one's particular misfortune are no longer available. Instead, one is left with one's blind and repressed anxieties – fears that grow and thrive in the very midst of ceaseless messaging and texting: as the always unsaid in the said, the constantly unaddressed in the address, the forever unformed in information. A dark side of words, therefore, which perpetually threaten to irrupt and tear conversation asunder, to draw speech itself into an unbridgeable abyss. If only a *human* voice was still there to tell us: "What you fear is what we all must fear. Communication and obliteration were always neighbors. You are not alone in seeing the dusk that dwells within words". But today this voice has been forgotten. Or, more precisely: it has drowned in the waves of general communication optimism and in the lighthearted spirit of exchanges in which we are all expected to take part. A brave new world of unending, unproblematic conversation with little room for hesitation and no room for skepticism and pessimism. The Promised Land is a land without darkness: Here where information flows like honey and everything is accessible to everyone, what need is there still for distrust and gloominess? Why look for problems where there aren't any? Why not rejoice instead? Yes, the pressure is on to smile and embrace: a metallic grin appropriate for the commencement of a new, second machine age. And while smartphones and iPads are venerated and celebrated like demigods, the shame of our doubtful, anxious, and hurting humanity can only grow stronger. No longer what connects us in our inescapable, existential solitude, it becomes the mark of disconnection in an otherwise perfectly connected, progressive world. The German thinker and philosopher, Günther Anders, had a specific name for this shame, for this self-contempt and self-reproached vulnerability. As he writes in one of his diary entries from 1942: "Believe I have found the signs of an entirely new pudendum this morning: a form of shame that did not exist in the past. I will provisionally call it *'Promethean shame'* for myself. I understand this to mean the *'shame when confronted by the humiliatingly high quality of fabricated things'*."[13] And as

Anders Kølle

Anders further explains: "Anyone who has never blundered while handling a machine; anyone who has never incredulously looked back in disbelief at the assembly line that wordlessly keeps on moving... anyone who has never looked down at their hands in an alienated and bemused manner, at these clumsy instruments here, because their obsolescence and incorrigible incompetence have caused the fall from grace – this person does not know the shame that is the shame of today, the shame that erupts daily a thousand times over. Anyone who denies the existence of this form of shame does so only because to admit that we have come such a gloriously long way to arrive at the ability to be ashamed in front of things makes them blush with shame."[14] Surely, one must wonder, as Anders does, where our own inventions and ingenuity are leading us? Or, perhaps more accurately: *How* they are leaving us behind? To meet what destiny? To be rendered obsolete in which ways? For good reasons, Anders had not yet heard of Shannon's theorems, he did not know about the digital revolution to come. His concept of shame is therefore still related to human hands, to man's manual labor – not to his intellectual faculties, to his speech and his thoughts. The source of Anders' Promethean shame is, in other words, limited to our bodily incompetence, not our mental clumsiness and ineptitude. Hence so many more causes to blush today – to feel small and insignificant in the Age of Information and vis-à-vis the speed and magnitude of exchanges. After all, man's greatest pride was never his hands but his brain: *Homo sapiens* – the *wise* human beings, Earth's superior species and nature's prodigy child. But this superiority and ascendancy is becoming less and less believable, seems increasingly suspect or outright ridiculous. A genuine paradigm shift is reshaping our self-image and reconfiguring our role: The conqueror has engineered his own defeat by creating a machinery that is simply too complex for himself. He can no longer rule, he can no longer keep up – so sounds the refrain of the new, self-doubting and self-degrading narrative. If Shannon, even if only reluctantly, still kept man in the communicative loop, still at least represented and positioned him as *points* at the extremities of the information transmission, such courtesies and symbolic pleasantries are no longer deemed necessary. Here is an emblematic example of how the problem is put by two of today's engineers and entrepreneurs, Daniel Kellmereit and Daniel Obodovski: "The notion of removing humans from the equation and delegating more decision-making to machines is nothing new... Machines are often not only faster than humans, but also more accurate, and they dramatically minimize the chance of human error... Considering how much decision-making ability has already been given to machines and how much more is going to go that way, and considering the speed at which information flows from sensors and devices to the cloud, will humans be able to comprehend? Are humans the major limiting factor in the development...? And, more importantly, will humans be able to cope with all this information?"[15] Surely, the questions are purely rhetorical, the answers are already given: Not by chance but by necessity: For our own good it is time to back down and check out and leave the communication channels to the more deserving. The old reprimand: Shush, your father is talking! – will soon sound: Be quiet! Can't you see the machines are talking? In the very near future machine-to-machine communication will no longer need or want human involvement and human intervention and interpretation – not even as endpoints or final destinations. Everything works simply better and easier without us. Here, therefore, is how the updated and optimized version of Shannon's communication system looks: "Overall, the M2M technology ecosystem can be split into three major groups: data acquisition, data transport, and data analysis. Data acquisition is the device or hardware space – this is where data is being collected from various sensors and sent to the network. Examples are body sensors that measure pulse or calorie consumption, automotive OBD-II devices that measure car acceleration, and many others... After the data is collected, it is sent over a network; this is data transport... Data analysis is where the information that is collected from sensors and devices and transported over the network is being analyzed, interpreted, and acted upon... The major innovation that has radically changed the data analysis space is a new kind of architecture, software, and hardware that addresses the previous challenge of large data sets and how to capture, curate, store, search, analyze, and visualize all that data."[16] Although the primary function of each component and link in this optimized and updated communication structure remains fundamentally recognizable and identical to Shannon's, it is noteworthy that the name "communication system" is now replaced by a "M2M technology ecosystem" and that what is being transmitted in this "ecosystem" are no longer "messages" but "data". Why this new terminology if the general scheme and organization is unchanged? Why not retain the more familiar and understandable concepts? A provisional answer may sound: Because it is precisely no longer familiarity and recognition which is the aim. If Shannon still saw the need to address his readers and reach out to them in everyday language – before radically excavating and changing the accustomed meaning of such words as "message", and "information" – then rupture and alienation is in the description of pure machine communication no longer hidden behind a reassuring veil of familiarity but introduced from the very outset. We, the readers, the non-experts, are not *supposed* to feel comfortable and reassured in our encounter with this new world of tweeting and collaborating machines. We are *supposed* to lose our breath, to feel excluded, expelled – left behind in a determinate and destined way. For haven't we just learned: The future connection of machines begins with the disconnection of humans. Perfect communication between things requires the excommunication of man. Or, which amounts to the same: The talking of machines is grounded on the silence of humankind. Hence the need to part company and break away – to untie the bonds and shackles of the past. If Shannon's system was still somewhat ambiguous or lukewarm in its rejection of humanity – only hinted at it in a manner that could, by the most yearning, still be mistaken for love – the M2M ecosystem is a genuine and blunt break-up letter: "I do not desire you anymore! Do not come back." And so the distance is accentuated, the breaches and gaps, which

Anders Kølle

make any hope of a future reunion and reconciliation appear impossible: But don't blame yourself. It is not you who has changed. It is I. It is I who must now go my own way.

A deeper analysis is, however, necessary in order to comprehend *how* the ways between humanity and machine communication are parting. It seems much too vague and poorly explained to simply reduce it to a question of human slowness and lack of comprehension. For what is it more precisely that a priori deems man unfit for the development? Which road is it that he is in advance judged incapable of traveling? What is it more precisely that exceeds man's ability to collect, interpret, and understand? Let us begin by proposing a seemingly odd and provocative answer: It is nothing less than the world itself which has become too colossal and overwhelming for man. It is the world in its sheer quantity, magnitude, and abundancy which supersede the faculties and powers of man. The road he can no longer take, the road which is blocked for human beings and has become a dead end for human intelligence and thought, is the very pathway leading to a comprehension of the world we inhabit. What we are today being summoned to acknowledge, to accept as a given, as an inescapable fact, is that we *as humans* and thus as *limited beings*, as *defined* and *finite* beings, are from the hands of nature, in our determined biological constitution, unable to fathom what nature itself has produced and presents. Our finitude is, in other words, what we are called forth to meet and to confirm in face of the world as the unsurpassable and disqualifying hindrance to our continued supremacy and rule. Or, put in the most condensed and lapidary fashion: The world is *from now on* what we can no longer grasp and what must necessarily slip away: We, humans, are destined to lose our grip.

One might object that there is nothing unintelligible or strikingly odd about this statement – least of all provocative: Isn't the history of ideas already full of skeptics and pessimists regarding man's ability to comprehend and adequately represent the world? Hasn't Pyrrho, the ancient Greek philosopher, already taught us that knowledge of things is impossible and that mankind must assume an attitude of reserve? And yet, this is not precisely what the statement says. For we are not dealing here with a timeless and therefore eternal impotence of man but rather with a movement and a development *through which* humanity is becoming incapable and losing its grip: A historical change, in other words, which now forces man to test his own limits and recognize his own defeat. Hence the quandary: Why will that which was still governable yesterday be untamable and ungraspable tomorrow? Why has the world suddenly grown too big and moved into an unbridgeable distance? It is as if history, contrary to Hegel's philosophy and beliefs, has unexpectedly changed both its course and its effect: Tired of being a grand force of conjunction and synthesis, it is now compelled to dissolve and disperse instead. Or, as if man had fallen victim to a joke or a tease of cosmic proportions: leading him on for millennia with the prize of Absolute Knowledge and Spirit dangling in front of him – only to abruptly cut him off and move the award beyond reach. However, it is not in the philosophy

Anders Kølle

of Hegel but in the thinking of Kant that we find the most engaging and thought-provoking attempt to describe man's encounter with that which is too large, too forceful, too majestic to comply with the limits of human imagination and understanding. What Kant calls "the sublime" and attempts to present with this notion is nothing less than the unpresentable itself: The feeling of displeasure and pain evoked by man's feebleness and utter insignificance vis-à-vis nature's grandest and proudest productions: a mountain range, a roaring sea, the starry heavens above us. In all cases – albeit in different ways – a drama and a catastrophe is repeated which consists in the repulsion of reproduction and rejection of recognition: In front of the boundless and formless no concept is adequate and no representation is possible. What nature presents simply supersedes the synthesizing abilities of our imagination and the determining power of our understanding. This, however, does not mean that the drama and conflict are essentially external and fought in the open – man versus mountains, thought versus sea. Instead, the entire battle is internal, the combatants purely cognitive, and the defeat wholly withdrawn and concealed: In the range of his own faculties, man is now forced to meet their end – in the depth of his own gifts and talents he is pushed to find their flaw. And so the defeat is nothing but a discovery; the adversary nothing but his limits; and the loss nothing but his self-assurance and pride. What first appeared as the actual opponent – the majestic mountains, the untamable and destructive forces of the sea – is in fact only the occasion for human self-inspection and the mirror of his restrictions – not the genuine cause or the actual victor of the battle. Hence the reason of sublime displeasure and dissatisfaction lies entirely in the finitude of man himself: Along the borders of his tethered abilities a disheartening insight is born: There are barriers mankind shall never surmount and mysteries he shall never unravel: Of life's immeasurable horizons and widths man will know only its discernible shadow; of the universe's abundance of time man will have to settle for a brief moment on this earth: To amass the ocean only with a bucket, to quench a godlike thirst through a slender straw – such would be the human condition, such would be the inescapable decree issued with the authority of existence itself.

And yet, as well-known, this is not the entire story, this is not where all must come to an end: For Kant is not the author of philosophical tragedies nor is he a rooted and steadfast pessimist. And so, the very moment all hope is gone and man is forever locked inside his own ineptitude, tied to his own shortcomings, blinded by his own limits, Kant immediately comes to the rescue and offers mankind a surprising escape from the disheartening impasse. Here is the grand yet simple salvation: Humans are not only sensible creatures but also rational beings. What man is unable to represent with his imagination and grasp with his understanding, he can nevertheless surmount and contemplate as an idea. For whereas knowledge is restricted by the boundaries of experience and the finitude of concepts, human reason, human ideas, respect no such limitations. The ideas of reason are unburdened and free: Beyond the rigid laws and determinations of nature they reveal an infinite side of man:

Anders Kølle

"Reason in a creature is a faculty for extending the rules and aims of the use of all of its powers far beyond natural instinct, and it knows no boundaries to its projects".[17]

To know no boundaries, to be held back or restricted by nothing: This is where infinity and freedom meet and conjoin to raise man above the confines of the sensible world and the inhibitions of his animal existence and relieve him of the burden of his insufficiencies: Weightless thoughts; unstoppable, inexhaustible ideas – the infinite is reached before and beyond comprehension. Nothing seems quite as effortless – yet nothing about it is easily explained: A human power to think, a *Geistesvermögen*: Ideas arise – irresistibly, irreducibly – and thoughts wake up to their own exhaustlessness: No man may ever *know* the true expanse of the universe – and nevertheless his reason is able to conceive the unlimited *as an idea*. No person may resist and survive the relentless, raging storm – yet no force of nature can rob him of his inborn, unbounded freedom. In the end, beyond all sensible and knowable ends, the absolute is revealed as the true vocation of man – the unconditioned and supreme as his authentic goal. Hence the grand and irresistible Kantian reversal: Where man was initially blind and powerless, he now intuits the unsurpassable forces of his ideas; where man began as finite and restrained, he now grasps the infinite horizons of his being. And so, the sublime productions of nature – even its greatest, most majestic mountains and its vastest, most forceful and violent seas – must yield to an intelligence surmounting every limit, surpassing any restraint. In Kant's own, famous formulation: "Two things fill the mind with ever new and increasing admiration and reverence, the more often and more steadily one reflects on them: the starry heavens above me and the moral law within me... The first begins from the place I occupy in the external world of sense and extends the connection in which I stand into an unbounded magnitude with worlds upon worlds and systems of systems, and moreover into the unbounded times of their periodic motion, their beginning and their duration. The second begins from my invisible self, my personality, and presents me in a world which has true infinity but which can be discovered only by the understanding, and I cognize that my connection with that world (and thereby with all those visible worlds as well) is not merely contingent, as in the first case, but universal and necessary. The first view of a countless multitude of worlds annihilates, as it were, my importance as an animal creature, which after it has been for a short time provided with vital force (one knows not how) must give back to the planet (a mere speck in the universe) the matter from which it came. The second, on the contrary, raises my worth as an intelligence infinitely through my personality, in which the moral law reveals to me a life independent of animality and even of the whole sensible world..."[8] From the insignificant, diminutive place I physically occupy to the infinite worth of my inner self and my intellect: Between these two incommensurables the entire value and specificity of humanity arises: If the first describes my inevitable ignorance and annihilation, my predestined stupidity and death – the second delineates a promise of salvation: my recurrent rebirth in the supersensible realm of the absolute. If the first is a material loan from nature which I will one day have to pay back, the second is my unconditional autonomy beyond any indebtedness or bookkeeping bound to extinguish my light. I am finite, I am infinite; I owe everything and I owe nothing. Hence the paradox, indeed the schizophrenia, of Kant's vision of man: With one foot in the prison of time and the other in the freedom of the eternal, we are both gamblers who can never win, and winners who need never gamble: The mountain is big, the mountain is small, the storm is relentless and yet it cannot touch me. That is the dwarf and the giant who both live in the human soul: Timid and fearless humanity, overpowered and empowered creatures. When the dwarf strays off and thinks he can manage on his own, how suffocating reality quickly becomes! Nothing but restraints and closures in every direction and dimension. No thought ever leaves or disrupts the mind's dry and determinate mechanics. But when the giant walks off, tired of his tedious and uninspired companion – how swiftly life turns troublesome once again! For thoughts which know no limits, ideas without any gravity and constraint, make the mind gallop too hastily ahead: The end of this world, the end of all worlds are both reached and surpassed in a second. On the rooftop of the universe, the thought finds no companionship but itself. Great abstractions mean equally great abandonments: The free flight is soon burdened by its own infinite lightness: How the mind then dreams of returning to the slower and heavier realm of sensibility and experience, of simple concepts and determinate judgments. And so the dwarf and the giant need each other, cannot live without each other for very long: With imprisonment and suffocation at one extreme and detachment and pure abstraction at the other, the two unlikely companions must, despite all differences, *because* of all differences, find a way to cooperate. Or in strictly Kantian terms: As sensible as well as rational creatures we need laws as well as freedom, understanding as well as reason. Therein lies the richness of Kant's philosophy – the way he sought to make mankind rich: With a double citizenship and a passport valid for both the limited and the absolute, man may feel at home everywhere.

But now a new order and a far less generous viewpoint are being imposed which no longer allow us our free and facile mobility: The days where the leap between faculties, registers and realms was easily made are over – or so, we are told. Not because the fundamental abilities of humans have deteriorated or disappeared, but because our surroundings and our technologies are moving forward with an irresistible, insuppressible pace. To repeat the words of Kellmereit and Obodovski: "Considering how much decision-making ability has already been given to machines and how much more is going to go that way, and considering the speed at which information flows from sensors and devices to the cloud, will humans be able to comprehend? Are humans the major limiting factor in the development...? And, more importantly, will humans be able to cope with all this information?" As in Kant's analysis of the sublime, man is thus once again facing the challenge of forces and magnitudes beyond both his imagination and understanding: Something too powerful and too vast precludes the faculty of reproduction to create an

Anders Kølle

adequate image and hinders the faculty of recognition from applying the proper concept. But unlike Kant's analysis, the initial impotence of human sensibility is no longer succeeded by the omnipotence of human reason and the unquenchable spirit of human freedom. Instead, the new narrative and the new encounter with the sublime end precisely where Kant's philosophy took off and raised cognition above its inborn inhibitions and intolerable ineptitude. Removed are the Kantian lever and salvation, erased are the traces of a happy ending. Hence the dismembering and destruction of the philosophical ideal but also the resolution of its inherent paradox: Man need no longer feel schizophrenic or confused by his diplopia: There are not two households in the human soul, not two different forces and abilities or two alternating registers of thought. All ideas and cognitions fall invariably into one category – belong entirely to just one human ability and mode of operation. The mind is exclusively computational – that is: everything stops at the thresholds of the sensible. Beyond apprehension and recognition there is nothing. Thus man's double citizenship is annulled and his leap into freedom is effaced. Between Kant's two perspectives, between "a life independent of animality" and an existence limited to "the place I occupy in the external world" only the latter is retained. What is retained of Kant's vision of man is, in other words, solely the finite being, the creature which must "... after it has been for a short time provided with vital force... give back to the planet (a mere speck in the universe) the matter from which it came." Or to put it in yet another way: Human existence is now exclusively measured and judged from the perspective of the dwarf. It is the little man, the timid and insecure Lilliputian – not the free and self-reliant man – who alone defines the features of humankind. Likewise, it is undoubtedly the little man, the easily overpowered man, who feels obliged to take Obodovski's and Kellmereit's questions seriously and answer them with reverence. First question: "Considering the speed at which information flows from sensors and devices to the cloud, will humans be able to comprehend? Will humans be able to cope with all this information?" "Most likely not," answers the little man. "I don't think we will." Second question: "Are humans therefore the major limiting factor in this development today?" "Yes, yes," says the little man. "You are probably right. I do believe that we are standing in the way." And surely, the dwarf cannot answer otherwise: Deprived of his companion and the force to transcend the limits of his finite imagination and understanding the world is undoubtedly too big, the information too great, and the development too fast. What is lost in the transition from the Kantian sublime to the technological sublime is thus the very mental power which ensured man's fundamental pride and inviolability – the Kantian bulwark against human degradation and self-deprecation. The surplus value of being human, the unique *Geistesvermögen* of our species, is precisely what the technological sublime disclaims and destroys: The days are over where man was *more* than what could be exhaustively defined and described – his worth is no longer raised infinitely above his sensible existence but is instead trapped therein. No longer protected by the inexplicability and inexhaustibleness of his being, no longer an exception in the world and an enigma to himself, he stands naked and disarmed before the technological belittlement: "Please, do forgive me, but I am not able to keep up." But if the technological development and the technological sublime thus rob man of his inner giant and his innate pride, this, however, does not mean that the giant has altogether vanished. Instead it would seem that the giant has migrated and found a new home and a new life outside of man – a home where he no longer needs to cooperate and negotiate with his old and slow-witted companion, but where he can finally move freely and reign on his own. This home, this new promising land of the giant, this castle of uninhibited thought is, of course, the machine. The machine-castle, the computer-palace: Pure abstraction could hardly have found a better and more suitable residence. Here, where the only language spoken is endless sequences of 0s and 1s and where a message contains no meaning but only a binary choice, the sluggish realm of the sensible is bypassed once and for all. *In abstracto* the resistance of matter and finitude is finally overcome and the supersensible and unlimited actualized. And so the machine meets man as the externalization of everything which he himself once claimed to be: An omnipotent, supreme creation destined for the absolute. Although the machine therefore appears familiar as the objectification of man's previous inner worth and pride, it has at the same time moved unto an unbridgeable distance as a glorious exhibition of everything which man is not. Hence the feeling of ambivalence: the machine's, the computer's simultaneous remoteness and proximity:

superior yet recognizable, aloof yet acquainted. But first and foremost an acute and irrepressible sense of contrast and opposition: What separates man and machine is nothing less than the irreducible difference between the bounded and the unlimited, the particular and the universal. On one side, in the ring corner of humanity, thus, the tame and palsied mind of the dwarf, and in the other corner, on the side of technology, the daunting and awe-inspiring strength of the computer-giant. The outcome is determined in advance. The defeat of humanity appears inevitable. Hence the equally irrefutable truth of Obodovski's and Kellmereit's proclamation: Mankind does indeed stand in the way – cannot but be a limiting factor and a genuine bottleneck in the development. And with this truism, grounded on this human devaluation and defeat, based on this logic of the technological sublime, the main obstacle on the road to unconditional computerization and unlimited digitization is emphatically removed. From man's distrust of himself emerges his dependence on the machine. From man's self-induced degradation springs the computer's ecstatic elevation. As the science-fiction writer Vernor Vinge once predicted: "We will soon create intelligences greater than our own... When this happens, human history will have reached a kind of singularity, an intellectual transition as impenetrable as the knotted space-time of a black hole, and the world will pass far beyond our understanding."[19] The darkness of ignorance and the chains of inability lie ready for us in the future. And as the giant continues to leap forward with the speed of Moore's law, the shrinking of humanity occurs at an equally astounding pace: Which

Anders Kølle

problems can man still solve single-handedly? What confidence should humanity continue to enjoy? The shaky and nervous hands are only increasing in number: in the cockpits on our airplanes, in the laboratories of our scientists, in the consulting rooms of our doctors: across the entire spectrum of labor and professions the uneasiness is setting in: Aren't we humans simply too imperfect? The deeper we crawl into the shadows of the giant, the more injurious becomes the suspicion directed against ourselves. In the nightfall of self-confidence only our indebtedness glimmers forth: Man and machine – the being who owes everything and the object who owes nothing.

MAN THE PLAYER

Long before the emergence of autonomous cars and planes and several decades before the first personal computers arrived, the Jewish philosopher and mystic, Martin Buber, gave us these apocalyptic lines: " – Speaker, you speak too late. But a moment ago you might have believed your own speech; now this is no longer possible. For an instant ago you saw no less than I that the state is no longer led: the stokers still pile up coal, but the leaders merely *seem* to rule the racing engines. And in this instant while you speak, you can hear as well as I how the machinery of the economy is beginning to hum in an unwonted manner; the overseers give you a superior smile, but death lurks in their hearts. They tell you that they have adjusted the apparatus to modern conditions; but you notice henceforth they can only adjust themselves to the apparatus, as long as that permits it. Their spokesmen instruct you that the economy is taking over the heritage of the state; you know that there is nothing to be inherited but the despotism of the proliferating It under which the I, more and more impotent, is still dreaming that it is in command."[20] Today, we have indeed woken up from this dream: the human reverie of absolute governance is over. But we have only left one dream in order to enter another. The new dream, humanity's new phantasm, goes by different names: the Second Machine Age, the Fourth Industrial Revolution, the Industrial Internet, the Internet of Things. However, the kernel of the dream is unequivocal: In a world of ubiquitous computing and total automation, man's infinite burden of responsibility will finally be lifted. In the nearby future, all work will be done, all problems will be solved, by super-intelligent, interconnected, intercommunicating machines. Miniscule, wireless sensors embedded in everything around us will enable objects to work together and mutually monitor and assist each other. Nothing will be left unnoticed or unattended in a world where all things will have gained a voice. Total automation means unlimited vocalization: smart coffee machines and refrigerators who talk and trade information; connected garments, wardrobes, and washing machines engaged in endless, unabated exchanges. Even nature – once so distant in its silence, once so foreign and mysterious in its calm – will be driven out of the depths of secrecy and into the circuits of perpetual monitoring and speech. No mountain will be mute, no riverbed unaccounted for. Nature's new and involuntary tongues force all matter and existence into the same, artificial and digital glade: one all-encompassing stage of perfect transparency and total accumulation. In the words of the business and technology writer, Samuel Greengard: "What makes the Internet of Things so powerful is that it connects physical-first products and items to each other as well as connecting them to digital-first devices, including computer and software applications. This makes it possible for all these devices to interact on a group or multipoint basis and share data in real time... The sum of all this is the Internet of Everything... It represents a more evolved and advanced state where physical and digital worlds are blended into a single space."[21] Through the universalizing, totalizing language of digitization, all separate realms of existence must leave their old trenches

Anders Kølle

of incommensurability behind and assemble under the law and authority of the net. And it is precisely *because* there is no use of humans in this digital and automatized glade – *because* and not *despite* man's future, unmistakable obsoleteness, that engineers and entrepreneurs are thoroughly optimistic and exited. For as automation gradually releases us from the cumbersome burdens of production, from our traditional roles as workforce and providers, our time and energy will be freed to pursue other goals and seek much greater joys. Erik Brynjolfsson and Andrew McAfee provide following explanation: "We're heading into an era that won't just be different; it will be better, because we'll be able to increase both the variety and the volume of our consumption. When we phrase it that way – in the dry vocabulary of economics – it almost sounds unappealing. Who wants to consume more and more all the time? But we don't just consume calories and gasoline. We also consume information from books and friends, entertainment from superstars and amateurs, expertise from teachers and doctors, and countless other things that are not made of atoms. Technology can bring us more choice and even freedom."[22] Expelled from the tiresome labor pool, discharged from every factory floor and office building, superfluous mankind finds in his very inutility the key to his future happiness and satisfaction: Man's very insignificance may turn out to be his greatest wealth, human incapacity to be the beautiful liberator. Or in the condensed and precise formulation of Arthur C. Clarke: "The goal of the future is full unemployment, so we can play."[23]

As mankind thus moves from his previous and tedious responsibilities of production to the liberty of uninhibited consumption, the tired worker is reborn a free and lighthearted player. In the transition from "vita activa" to "vita contemplativa" the old concept of "homo ludens" now reemerges to reshape and redefine the role of humankind. Man the Player replaces Man the Maker. Henceforth, the grand purpose of humans shall no longer be tied to what they build and construct, but to how they cherish and enjoy. Idle men will once again look beautiful and attractive: closer to the fresh complexion of carefree children than to the troubled and sad demeanor of the old working class. And together with man's rejuvenation the entire world is refreshed and renewed: no longer a place of duty, no longer a prison of commitment, everywhere and everything welcomes man to play. Who, then, will miss their former offices and their prior assignments, meetings, and responsibilities? Were they ever more than a necessary evil in a world too often deprived of joy? Perhaps one should even ask: Isn't it only now, at this moment, that man fulfils his true destiny as nature's privileged and playful son? Among others, Oscar Wilde once believed so: "... just as trees grow while the country gentleman is asleep, so while Humanity will be amusing itself, or enjoying cultivated leisure – which, and not labour, is the aim of man – ... machinery will be doing all the necessary and unpleasant work."[24] And the great poet and playwright, Friedrich Schiller, gave this idea an even more forceful and condensed expression. Already at the early dawn of industrialization Schiller wrote these famous words: "For to declare it once and for all, Man plays *only when he*

Anders Kølle

is in the full sense of the word a man, and he is only wholly Man when he is playing."[25] To these writers "homo ludens" is thus the very essence of humanity, the eternal kernel and true spirit of man which monotonous and uninspired work has only occulted and distorted. Although none of them could have foreseen the outbreak and impact of the digital revolution, they were in their own idiosyncratic ways already addressing the questions and looking for the answers to a radically changed and modernized society. They too could see the hopelessness and claustrophobia of a life increasingly determined by production: the tyranny of utility, the one-sidedness of instrumental reason. How foreign and graceless humans become when existence is reduced to one single function! How void of any spirit and brightness! Industrialization meant specialization and specialization in turn meant fragmentation. Modern work cut through the minds and bodies of people and forced them to accept their own mutilation: Amputated souls in mistreated bodies filled the growing cities with their half-wit and half-dreams and limping imagination. That is why the words "full" and "whole" are of special significance to Schiller. To play means first of all to complete: to heal what modern life and work has ripped apart: imagination, reason, feeling, memory, understanding. Free play is what allows all faculties and talents, all human registers and emotions to enter into relations and create new constellations: the building, the "*Bildung*", of a still more beautiful and consolidated man. Autonomy and self-creation thus stand over against thralldom through fragmentation. If the latter demands people to be entirely

satisfied with what is only half, the former compels people
to be fully *un*satisfied unless they are truly whole. Only thus
can the immanent and imminent disasters of modernization
and industrialization be prevented. Modern work versus
free play marks the difference between humanity losing
itself in the grip of progress, withering in the midst of
flowering production, and the realization of human's inner
strength and freedom. Much too easy to get run over by the
development, it demands true stamina and great sincerity to
remain light and joyful enough to play. Only the careless and
foolish take play lightly – the thoughtful know how essential
and truly serious it is.

With these accounts it is difficult to imagine a more
passionate defense of "homo ludens": In all of the above
examples, Man the Player is lifted from the sad periphery of
pointless pastime and meaningless distraction and into the
very center of human existence: Man should be known by
the way he plays – not by the tedious and tiresome work he
performs. What is less certain, however, is whether there is
also absolute agreement on the very concept and meaning of
play. Does play denote the same thing and contain the same
promise to all the authors? Or is it really quite different how
Schiller and McAfee or Wilde and Clarke perceive it? It is
difficult to overlook at least one big difference: When Schiller
dreams of the perfect man, he is still thinking of a powerful
and endless being. Schiller's player remains a creature and
creator of the supersensible and the eternal. Or more
precisely: It is man's very ability to access and inhabit both
the sensible realm and the supersensible that makes playing

Anders Kølle

possible in the first place: To play is a coupling of the material and the spiritual, of the finite and the infinite, by which man acknowledges and embraces his dual, composite nature. This is how Schiller's player becomes a fulfilled and whole human being. What he plays with is his own riches and talents – and what he wins is his self in its vast and unbroken dimensions. The affinities between Schiller and Kant are therefore quite obvious: Man's inner worth is raised infinitely through the true depths and majestic range of his being: Reaching from the temporal and determinate to the ecstatic heights of the eternal, man is indeed a cosmic child with the entire universe as his playground. But, as we have tried to show in the previous, it is precisely this very sublimity, this human greatness and ineffable *Geistesvermögen*, which appear highly questionable or outright impossible today. In the age of digitization, at the dawn of ubiquitous computing and automation, man is no longer so much a cosmic child and a universal player but rather a reprimanded and admonished child, who is forced to recognize his own limitations – which is also to say: man's playground is no longer immeasurable but reduced to the size of his finite and frail understanding. It is now in the corner that man must play – in the shadows and under the supervision of the computer-giant: the all-seeing nanny of the Information Age. All of which prompts the question: What is humanity now to play? What sort of games and toys is belittled and demystified man to enjoy? In which direction should he seek his pleasures? To turn inward seems a bad idea that would only lead to disappointment and disillusion: Purely sensible and cornered creatures are no great promise of fun! How definitely the days are over when we, in Hoffmann's words, could still hope to find an "inexhaustible diamond mine within ourselves."[26] Or in which a Romanticist like Novalis was able to wonder: "Is not the universe within ourselves? The depths of our spirit are unknown to us... The mysterious way leads inward."[27] Surely, "bottlenecks" have no such mysteries – nor any inner diamond mine yet uncovered. Disenchanted, devalued humanity must remain on the sober side of self-aggrandizement and self-intoxication. And so, there is in truth only one way to go, only one direction to take the game and the fun: outward. And this is precisely where the technological sublime and the Internet of Things are ready to bring us to. To repeat Brynjolfsson's and McAfee's prediction: "We're heading into an era that won't just be different; it will be better, because we'll be able to increase both the variety and the volume of our consumption... Technology can bring us more choice and even freedom." And as the two authors continue: "When... things are digitized – when they're converted into bits that can be stored on a computer and sent over a network – they acquire some weird and wonderful properties. They're subject to different economics, where abundance is the norm rather than scarcity."[28] In the digital age, the true treasures and wonders exist online, in the infinity of possibilities and abundance of choices provided by the net. Which is also to say: the "inexhaustible diamond mine" is no longer to be sought in the depths and intricacies of the human mind but in the exuberance and boundlessness of bits and data. Too unimaginative and impoverished to entertain ourselves, too

Anders Kølle

miserably and profoundly bored with our own limits and finitude, the fun and the games must come from outside. Or to put it plainly: consumption is the name of man's best game. Instead of starving on our own meager resources we feast on the abundance of excitement online; instead of groping in the dimness of our exhausted imagination, we are steered by the steady, serene computer-lights: Playing has never been easier, consumption never quicker. Existence reaches an ecstatic pace in the digital currents of immaterial, ephemeral choices and goods. As driftwood we are carried hastily forward, riding on the ripples and waves of the digital sea. An oceanic feeling, indeed: As vast, immeasurable, and engulfing as the endless internet itself. Online consumers thus consume and *are consumed*: Consume to *be consumed*! To be carried astray, still further out and away – absorbed, swallowed up on the all-welcoming and all-eating surface of inconsequential choices and dreams. Here we, the dwarfs, have the chance to momentarily surpass and forget ourselves: to experience a lighter life – a life less burdened by the dreariness of our limited visions and understanding – and become part of a virtual and absolute greatness. In short: We go online to play with the giant and meet the sublime. Or in the words of an anonymous teenager in an interview with the American author and psychologist, Sherry Turkle: "I feel that I am part of a larger thing, the Net, the Web. The world. It becomes a thing to me, a thing I am part of. And the people, too, I stop seeing them as individuals, really. They are part of this larger thing."[29] Participation, then, is the most adequate name of the digital game. The lost pride and dignity is re-captured through affiliation: The grandeur and infinitude rub off on the finite, the unlimited casts its celestial light on the bounded, the sublime moves once again within reach. And yet, this affiliation and intoxication is strictly one-sided, exclusively one-directional: As little as the sea cares for its driftwood and surfers, just as little does the internet tend to and commit to the individual user. Beneath the liberating rush of the ride and the dreamy endlessness of free choices hide, therefore, a deeper and less agreeable reality and truth: our individual impotence and insignificance vis-à-vis the infinity we so admire. The digital fun and games, the internet's sea of excitement and possibilities, remains an outer and purely virtual possession and reality: the sublime is not in us but beyond us, not ours but its own. As nothing but drifters and surfers only the trajectories – not the seascape – are under our control and command. Tied to surfaces – not released into depths – restricted to an outward search – not an inner journey and exploration – we are left with purely superficial choices and only a fleeting and flickering sense of autonomy. Nothing in the technological sublime nurtures or raises our inner worth or propagates a more than evanescent freedom. On the contrary, we must play and consume by the online rules: the game of externalization and commercialization – the depthless game of unilateral participation and instant gratification: on the web only surface-dreams and surface-thoughts are possible: Everything has to be immediately accessible, directly expressible – brought into its most skirting and shimmering dimension: Merchandise for the eyes and minds, snapshots and stimuli for the comprehension. In the description of another of Sherry Turkle's teenagers: "If I'm upset, right as I feel upset, I text a couple of my friends… just because I know that they'll be there and they can comfort me. If something exciting happens, I know that they'll be there to be excited with me, and stuff like that. So I definitely feel emotions when I'm texting, as I'm texting… Even before I get upset and I know that I have that feeling that I'm gonna start crying, yeah, I'll pull up my friend."[30] Answering the demand for perpetual sharing and exteriorization, playing by the rules of instant consumption and gratification, thoughts and feelings can be nothing but ripples and foam on an ever-moving sea. Deprived of any sense of inner and deeper reservoirs or breadths, of any interior capacities and strengths, the surface becomes the sole plane of cognition and recognition: online existence must constantly evaluate, empty and evacuate itself – there simply seems to be no alternative, no possibility of holding down and holding back. Schiller's cosmic and wholesome child now seems to have turned into an irruptive and bulimic teenager: outward is the direction everything must take: Every minor dream and sensation, every single thought and frustration: Even the lightest mental content is now too big and too cumbersome for the fragile and easily capsized self of the web. Emotions are therefore deemed to remain unformed and premature: A disoriented vibration, a groping and uncertain sensation. And thoughts are interrupted and disgorged well before they gain weight and complexity, before they turn ripe, forceful, and rich – and much too heavy to bear. A new and involuntary shallowness is the inevitable result of this ceaselessly ejecting and abortive mind: given neither time nor room for growth, ideas and dreams are flung half-fledged and helpless overboard and into the communicative and digital sea: Like wreckage words and utterances shimmer for a moment on the surface before they sink beneath the thresholds of attention and into collective and eternal oblivion. This is clearly no longer a matter of freedom of speech or of any drive to expression. Rather expressiveness is the inevitable outcome and debris of a distressed mind unable to internalize and hold on to a single feeling: impoverishment not empowerment is the source of the ever-increasing and feverish communication. Not surprisingly, it is, however, the exact opposite which we are commonly told. In the words of the social media-master, Mark Zuckerberg: "I think that people just have this core desire to express who they are. And I think that's always existed."[31] And as Zuckerberg continues: "… we built Facebook around a few simple ideas. People want to share and stay connected with their friends and the people around them. If we give people control over what they share, they will want to share more. If people share more, the world will become more open and connected. And a world that's more open and connected is a better world. These are still our core principles today."[32] How compellingly easy and cheerful this sounds. How unquestionably good! We recognize in the words of Zuckerberg the same, unshakeable optimism which also steers the discourse and mindset of Brynjolfsson and McAfee: We are heading towards a better future. Technology will bring us more choices and more freedom. Through increased consumption and communication, through incessant sharing and participation, the human condition is constantly improved. Whether the final aim is absolute openness and transparency or uninhibited choices and play, the means remain identical: externalization and dissemination of every single drive and desire: Existence must turn outward and into expression in order to liberate itself. And with this general guideline for an ameliorated life, in this rush of enthusiasm on humanity's behalf, there seems to be little or no need for further inquiries and doubt. Least of all for the questions most pertinent to us: what is the significance of the withhold breath? Of dreams and ideas that dwell before they are awakened – grow in silence before they are expressed and spoken? The profundity of feeling, the depths of our sensitive and imaginative being: Do we really travel better without them? And how much of this journey can still be called free?

FREEDOM AND DATA

We must return, therefore, to the concept and conditions of freedom in the computerized, digitized world. If the concept of freedom has never been easy to tackle and has too often been misused as the spearhead and magic word for anything but liberating ideologies and forces – each century with its own political and philosophical interpretations and violations – then the concept appears no less ambiguous and in a new and paradoxical way restrained in the digital age. But let us first reiterate and recall what freedom supposedly means and wherein it seemingly consists for the contemporary subject: Above all, it is a freedom of consumptive choice and a freedom of digital expression enabled and ensured by swift and increasingly ubiquitous computation. Instant accessibility and unending availability are here the two overlapping and crucial principles guiding the development. A development which is, let's not forget, made possible by the immateriality of the goods and services themselves – or by what, Brynjolfsson and McAfee called the "weird and wonderful properties" of digitized things. Since we no longer consume atoms but bits, no longer disseminate matter and print, our online existence and liberty is a priori shielded from the ties of exhaustibility and limits of availability framing and steering traditional economics and conventional market logics. Abundance is therefore the name of the rupturing and emancipating force providing hitherto unthinkable possibilities for our online selves. As such, this digital liberation may adequately be described and rubricized as a *positive liberty* since its main aim and significance consist in the empowerment of the individual to choose, act, and express herself according to her free will, opinion, and desires. The freedom granted by the internet is, in short and when regarded from this perspective, freedom for self-realization.

If the first concept of freedom thus centers on abundance and on individual action, the second type we have encountered derives, on the other hand, from seeming passivity and absence. This is the freedom *from* restraints and absence of impediments which a future of ubiquitous computing and total automation has promised to grant humanity. Ideally and ultimately by releasing man altogether from his previous burdens of work and productivity, thus freeing him to lead a carefree life of leisure and enjoyment instead. Or to repeat the words of Arthur C. Clarke: "The goal of the future is full unemployment, so we can play." As distinct from the first concept of liberty, we may define this second type as a *negative liberty*, since its value lies less in any positively defined possibilities or acquisitions than in the disappearance or annulation of external constraints: *Not* to work, *no longer* to be subjected to the hitherto unquestionable necessity and imperative of labor, constitute *eo ipso*, the negative foundation of this new emancipation. Freedom results thus from an abolition rather than an attainment. Man distinguishes himself by what he *doesn't* need to do, *doesn't* need to be, and seeks his joy and fulfilment in this very void and lack.

In the previous, we have sought to question these liberties

by putting them in a different and far less generous light: Not with the purpose to expect less from the development and the future but in order for us to demand more of emancipated man. In the shadows cast by strong digital euphoria and stark technological ambition we find the remnants of broken humanistic dreams and of abandoned humanistic values: Principles and propositions no longer applicable to the new digital reality. But we also find new forms of human servility and serfdom taking shape and gaining strength in the very midst of our new freedoms. Neither the dreams of unhindered consumption and unlimited expression nor the call for a free and jobless existence are quite as unambiguous and gratuitous as commonly portrayed: Both the positive and the negative liberties foster their own shadow pictures and produce their own pitfalls and risks: Each liberty has its dangers, each freedom its costs. Hence the importance and urgency of the question: Who or what will the digital era set free? What will technologically emancipated man become?

To us the greatest risks are unquestionably tied to the digital devaluation and demystification of man: The technological dismissal of human reason and imagination – the degradation of man's inner world and worth. Divorced from his mental depths and riches mankind seems to pay for his future liberation with the increased restraining and limitation of his mind. This resembles less the birth of a free and inventive seer but rather the emergence of a new vulnerability: Disarmed is man's encounter with the computer, disempowered his relation to the machine. As the finite must surrender in front of the infinite, so must man recede vis-à-vis the machine. His tool has outgrown him, its progress overpowered him: Unending perfectability and unlimited potentiality are now hopes associated uniquely with the technological and digital sphere. But more than pride is lost in the process: For which freedoms are built on superfluity and what liberties have play as their only aim? Is the dismissed truly emancipated and the belittled happy with his endless games? There seem to be genuine reasons to worry on behalf of humanity: Once immeasurability and infinity are no longer gracing and dignifying the human mind and soul, once the supersensible is no more an attainable end of human dreams and thought, man is inevitably forced into regressive and reclusive circles – centripetal motions of inescapable self-doubt and self-reproach. Surely, one might consider this disrobing and disqualification as nothing but a timely and necessary response to centuries of absurd, human self-aggrandizement and self-celebration: Hasn't it become all too obvious that man has done a bad job ruling this earth? That his time in front and in command has been an age of veritable terror? And that therefore, it is far better, more sensible really, to place man emphatically on the side of the finite, the perishable, and the negligible? In response, it ought to be remembered that in man's depths and infinitude, in his faculties of reason and imagination, lie more than a simple tool and excuse for domination and oppression: Human immeasurability is also the true bulwark *against* abuse and exploitation: Only to the extent that we are perpetually more than what can be circumvented and exhaustively described, only in our capacity to ceaselessly transgress against and overflow all conceptual stratifications and linguistic simplifications, does our existence remain beyond the traps of objectification. It is as limitless and inexhaustible beings that we escape the reduction to a means. It is as infinite and indeterminate creatures that we remain more than a thing. This inner worth of unending and immeasurable proportions provides us with the fundamental inviolability which persists and resists the ongoing onslaughts of instrumentalization and effectivization. The inexplicable and unspeakable excesses or surpluses are therefore not only dispensable garlands and extravagant coronals awarded to a vain and lavish humanity. Nor are they superfluous fantasies and unfruitful fabrications of purely delusional minds. On the contrary, they are essential as the individual's main protection from the calculative forces of exploitation always ready to enslave new subjects. Hence we must shun any attempts at reducing or annulling the inner vastness of man. And to the extent that the technological sublime causes precisely such destructions, there is every reason to be wary of its victorious and unchallenged march. One must, in other words, be sensitive to the violations inside the possibilities and liberations promised by our digital age: The birth of a reality in which we play no longer as cosmic children but as corrected and superfluous infants in a world governed from outside. A world in which our expressions of freedom and freedoms of expression are no more than an inconsequential shimmering on the surface of a self-monitoring, autarchic actuality.

These dangers and the nature of this exigency become still more obvious once we turn our attention towards the true technological foundation of the digital age: data. Indeed, all the advancements and liberties promised by the new age hinge on the use and accumulation of data. Both the positive liberty to make endless consumer choices and the negative liberty to experience complete joblessness would be utterly unthinkable without the constant collection and ceaseless dissemination of gigantic amounts of data. Data is what passes from machine to machine in the automated world of the industrialized internet and data is what enables our computers to offer us inexhaustible amounts of digital choices and digital goods. All digital and smart technologies rely on it and so do, consequently, still more consumers, still more vendors and businesses and a still greater part of our well-fare, politics and economies. In the lapidary formulation of Samuel Greengard: "At the most basic level the IoT and Industrial Internet are about data and extracting value from it."[33] And as the American futurist and entrepreneur, Martin Ford, explains: "The ever-growing mountain of data is increasingly viewed as a resource that can be mined for value – both now and in the future. Just as extractive industries like oil and gas continuously benefit from technical advances, it's a good bet that accelerating computer power and improved software and analysis techniques will enable corporations to unearth new insights that lead directly to increased profitability. Indeed, that expectation on the part of investors is probably what gives data-intensive companies like Facebook such enormous valuations."[34] Data is, in other words, the main asset of the

Anders Kølle

emerging digital economies: what oil- and coal-reserves were to the industrialized world of analog machines, data and data sets are destined to become to the postindustrial future of digital and ubiquitous computing. Governments', businesses' and organizations' ability to tap into multiple sources of data and to process and apply this data efficiently and intelligently will make the difference between future success and failure. Data harvested and collected from anything from vending machines, television sets, parking meters, and gas pumps to food packages, light switches, supermarket shelves, and restrooms, provides comprehensive insights into the specific needs, preferences and behavioral patterns of citizens and customers alike. A hitherto unthinkable level of precision in the way individuals are summoned, targeted, or served is now made possible. In the description by Martin Ford: "Major retailers are relying on big data to get an unprecedented level of insight into the buying preferences of individual shoppers, allowing them to make precisely targeted offers that increase revenue while helping them to build customer loyalty. Police departments across the globe are turning to algorithmic analysis to predict the times and locations where crimes are most likely to occur and then deploying their forces accordingly... Tools that provide new ways to visualize data collected from social media interactions as well as sensors built into doors, turnstiles, and escalators offer urban planners and city managers graphic representations of the way people move, work, and interact in urban environments, a development that may lead directly to more efficient and livable cities."[35]

With correct, sufficient data there is money and time to be saved in almost every branch and aspect of service, business, and governance. And the larger the data sets and the better the algorithms become, the greater is also the ability to move beyond the representations and thresholds of the immediate and towards reliable predictions of the future. Predictive analytics is the name of this data-based prophesizing designed to identify and comprehend events well before they take place. This encompasses not only the premonition and reporting of natural occurrences and environmental catastrophes such as earthquakes, floods, and droughts, but also the ability to foresee much less dramatic events: a consumer's likely choices and dispositions, a customer's desire to change bank or insurance company – to buy a new house or sell an old car. Due to sophisticated, self-correcting algorithms and an exponential growth of sensors and data points, the future appears still more foreseeable and calculable, still more transparent and unequivocal: no longer the unknown and ungovernable par excellence it is lured ever closer to the snares and circumscriptions of ubiquitous computing. In space as well as time, in private as well as public, data are unlocking secrets and opening the gateways to vast and previously unthinkable colonizations: the colonization of the possible, the domestication of the next. As a giant repository of computable risks and measurable gains, the coming and the possible are framed and orchestrated up front – made answerable and amenable to predictions tapping the future in advance. Hence the possible is in a strange way made necessary and the next is paradoxically and continuously delayed: Algorithms have

Anders Kølle

already provided the answers, big data already uncovered and summoned the truth.

It is certainly not difficult to imagine how these superhuman insights and capabilities may very quickly jeopardize or violate fundamental human liberties and rights. Most obvious among them is surely the individual's right to privacy. In a world where almost everything is constantly monitored, recorded, and analyzed it becomes an increasingly onerous if not impossible task to shield and sustain any private realm or domain. Not only our actions and behavior but also our intimate feelings, desires, and thoughts are subject to aggressive surveillance and computation due to the penetrating and pervasive forces of data-analytical software and tools. Martin Ford recounts the following, illustrative story: "The US superstore chain, Target, Inc., provided a... controversial example of the ways in which vast quantities of extraordinarily detailed customer data can be leveraged. A data scientist working for the company found a complex set of correlations involving the purchase of about twenty-five different health and cosmetic products that were a powerful early predictors of pregnancy. The company's analysis could even estimate a woman's due date with a high degree of accuracy. Target began bombarding women with offers for pregnancy-related products at such an early stage that, in some cases, the women had often not yet shared the news with their immediate families. In an article published in early 2012, the *New York Times* reported one case in which the father of a teenage girl actually complained to store management about mail sent to the family's home – only to find out later that Target, in fact, knew more than he did."[36] The level of intrusion and absurd privacy violation is here directly proportional to the available quantity of personal data and the identification of a series of essential predictors. And as the amount of produced and accumulated data in these years is growing at an exponential rate – doubling roughly every three years – such violations may before long become the rule rather than the exception. Indeed, one should ask: How soon before algorithms predict pregnancies even prior to the women themselves? But what Martin Ford's example also shows is something which, in truth, goes well beyond the pure question of privacy rights and privacy issues: what it foretells as a sign, as an early symptom and premonition, is nothing less than the entry into a new and very curious reality. A reality which is, in fact, the very opposite of natality and birth but instead the premature termination of all kinds of pregnancy. For what predictive analytics and big data seem all too eager to produce is an inescapable world of pre-established, pre-calculated, and pre-orchestrated events – a factual and unfertile actuality incapable of producing and giving birth to true potentiality and to the genuinely unexpected: the future carries no longer the promise of the eternally unforeseen, is no longer pregnant with the utterly fortuitous and the startlingly unanticipated. On the contrary, a reality steered and controlled by data is a reality governed by the already given, by facts and figures which can be no different, which offer no difference, but exhaust themselves entirely in their representations and expositions. And indeed, this is precisely what the word *data* essentially means: derived from the Latin noun *datum* it signifies a "(thing) given" – neuter past participle of the Latin verb *dare* "to give". As something *given* – or, more originally, as the gesture and act of *giving* itself – we should adequately think of *data* as a gift: a present in the form of a presentation. What data gives is a thing *as it presently is*. The gift consists in this very *giving* which delivers and discloses the being of something making it stand forth. We can say that data in truth *ex-poses* in the sense of both exhibiting and bringing to a halt. The being of the given thing can no longer be *anything* but only what the exposition fixates and shows. Hence the certainty and inevitability which naturally accompany all data: For surely a thing can only be what it is! Nothing could be more obvious! What is far less evident, however, is what data simultaneously withdraws or hides: the possibility of an alterity beyond what is presently given and at hand – something completely other than what is exposed and brought to a halt. Herein lies the invisible poverty of the presented gift, the inevitable barrenness of the purely actual: Data can only give the thing as necessity, as this or that indisputable fact – not as potentiality, not as natality. It speaks solely of a world that must be but remains insensitive and blind to the things that *could* be. The objective world of data is in this sense a stifled reality: always called on to deliver facts, always required to conform to purely presentational demands, it is caught in its own mesh of ubiquitous exposition and transparency. To perpetually present the gift of the present, to continuously give itself up to acquisition, it exhausts itself in incessant delivery and unending externalization. In other words: This is not a world that hopes, not a world that neither fabulates nor envisions. Factual reality is a firm administrator which accepts no adventurous divergences or unaccounted digressions: "Content yourself with the given" – such sounds the credo of the factually-steered actuality.

How inevitable! How inescapable! How quickly and surely any idea or concept of freedom is darkened by this unreturnable gift of the present. For freedom thrives not in the given, prospers not surrounded by actuality and facts. As transgression of the immediate and transcendence of the factual freedom is in its very essence opposed to "the given thing." Thus nothing could be further from freedom than for it to "content itself". And nothing is less in the spirit of emancipation than the ceaseless confirmation of the real. On the most basic and essential level data and freedom are bound to bump heads: One always pointing to the necessary, the other always calling for possibility or absence of restraint. Hence the two distinct claims they make on the world: surrender yourself to the present or present a possibility to go beyond. However, this conflict and contradiction isn't *per se* destructive, doesn't need to lead to battle and mutual eradication. Not, at least, in a multifarious and miscellaneous world – not as long as thinking and existence provides sufficient room for both. In the past, such encompassing, embracing largess has commonly been the goal. Indeed, we might even ask: What science, what philosophy, what art has not sought to somehow balance and negotiate between the two? To find room in the given for the new and find basis for the new in the given. Where such thinking succeeds it opens up necessity to possibility and finds in the possible the seeds of necessity and grains of gravity that can make the possible real. We may call this the grounding of the possible and the leaping of the given. Each of the two opponents invigorates and develops the other. But in a future governed increasingly by data the force of this dialectic is bound to diminish – or even altogether disappear. Instead of multifariousness we get unchallenged monotony unable to harbor more than the actual and the given. This is the very frigidity of a completely monitored and wholly analyzed and recorded world: precisely the world promised by ubiquitous computing and the internet of everything. Compared to this largescale violation of the possible and this encroachment on the essence of freedom, the positive and negative liberties of our promised digital future seem very pale and insignificant. Based on the exchange of bits and data, enabled by sensors and automation, the free choices of consumption and the freedom to be unemployed are born from the very authority and supremacy of the actual, which fundamentally impairs the spirit of freedom. With these liberties we seem therefore to receive nothing more than a surveyed and administered emancipation: freedoms besieged by inevitability, possibilities permeated by necessity: Purely superficial liberties, therefore, which are unable to escape the commandment of the present and challenge the rule of the given. Beneath the veils of liberty seems instead to hide a new and ever-deeper kind of dependency: our growing need of computers to govern the world *as it is*. Big data requires giants – not a belittled humanity.

NOTES

[1] Karl Marx, Friedrich Engels: *The Communist Manifesto* (Stanford: Pluto Press, 2017)

[2] Claude E. Shannon, Warren Weaver: *The Mathematical Theory of Communication* (Chicago: University of Illinois Press, 1963), 31

[3] Ibid., 8

[4] Ibid., 27

[5] Ibid., 34

[6] Ibid., ix

[7] Norbert Wiener: *Cybernetics: or Control and Communication in the Animal and the Machine* (Cambridge: The MIT Press, 1965), 61

[8] Bernard Stiegler: *Symbolic Misery, Volume 2: The Catastrophe of the Sensible* (Cambridge: Polity Press, 2015), 64-65

[9] Ibid., 75

[10] Ibid., 75

[11] Claude E. Shannon, Warren Weaver: *The Mathematical Theory of Communication* (Chicago: University of Illinois Press, 1963), 25

[12] Bernard Stiegler: *Symbolic Misery, Volume 2: The Catastrophe of the Sensible* (Cambridge: Polity Press, 2015), 73

[13] Günther Anders: "On Promethean Shame", in: *Prometheanism: Technology, Digital Culture and Human Obsolescence* (London: Rowman & Littlefield International, 2016), 30

[14] Ibid., 87

[15] Daniel Kellmereit, Daniel Obodovski: *The Silent Intelligence: The Internet of Things* (San Francisco: DnD Ventures, 2013), 48-49

[16] Ibid., 30-32

[17] Paul Guyer: *Kant* (London: Routledge, 2006), 416

[18] Ibid., 1-2

[19] Erik Brynjolfsson, Andrew McAfee: *The Second Machine Age: Work, Progress, and Prosperity in A Time of Brilliant Technologies* (New York: W.W. Norton, 2014), 254-255

[20] Martin Buber: *I and Thou* (New York: Touchstone, 1996), 97

[21] Samuel Greengard: *The Internet of Things* (Cambridge: The MIT Press, 2015), 18

[22] Erik Brynjolfsson, Andrew McAfee: *The Second Machine Age: Work, Progress, and Prosperity in A Time of Brilliant Technologies* (New York: W.W. Norton, 2014), 9-10

[23] Ibid., 178

[24] Nicholas Carr: *The Glass Cage: Who Needs Humans Anyway?* (London: Vintage, 2015), 25

[25] Friedrich Schiller: *On the Aesthetic Education of Man* (New Haven: Yale University Press, 1954), 80

[26] Rüdiger Safranski: *Romanticism: A German Affair* (Evanston: Northwestern University Press, 2014), 152

[27] Ibid., 72

[28] Erik Brynjolfsson, Andrew McAfee: *The Second Machine Age: Work, Progress, and Prosperity in A Time of Brilliant Technologies* (New York: W.W. Norton, 2014), 10

[29] Sherry Turkle: *Alone Together* (New York: Basic Books, 2011), 168

[30] Ibid., 175

[31] George Beahm: *The Boy Billionaire* (Chicago: Agate Publishing, 2012), 59

[32] Ibid, 67

[33] Samuel Greengard: *The Internet of Things* (Cambridge: The MIT Press, 2015), 54

[34] Martin Ford: *The Rise of the Robots: Technology and the Threat of Mass Unemployment* (London: Oneworld Publications, 2015), 91

[35] Ibid., 89-90

[36] Ibid., 90

CONTRIBUTORS

Anders Kølle is an art historian with a Ph.D. from The European Graduate School. He currently teaches art history at the University of Copenhagen, Denmark, with special focus on modern art and its methodology. He is the author of several books on art, technology, and science including the titles *Beyond Reflection*, *Two Be or Not Two Be* and *The Work of Art – Its Process of Becoming*.

Sarah and Schooling is a two-woman graphic design studio based in Singapore. They connect ideas, visualise concepts, and develop design strategies that best communicate the needs and objectives of their clients. An ardent supporter of Singapore's literary scene, the studio is actively involved in designing books and publications across multiple genres. Their capabilities and experience stretch beyond publications, reaching other creative disciplines such as visual identity and branding, art directing, editorial design, web design, copywriting, and conducting workshops.